Gladys Nicol

MALAYSIA
and
SINGAPORE

B. T. Batsford Ltd *London*

Dedication
To the Tan Clan

First published 1977
© Gladys Nicol 1977
ISBN 0 7134 0839 1

Printed in Great Britain by
J. W. Arrowsmith Ltd., Bristol
for the publishers
B. T. Batsford Ltd.,
4 Fitzhardinge Street,
London W1H 0AH

Contents

Illustrations

Acknowledgments

It is impossible to list all the people who have contributed to the pages of this book. Most of them are scattered across the face of the globe, in Canada, India, Australia, Britain and Europe, as well as within Malaysia and in Singapore. They all gave it life and my sincere thanks go to them.

Among them though, are a few who have really made it possible for me to attempt to cover this very large area of South-East Asia, and my special thanks are due to them. Thai International and the Tourist Organisation of Thailand arranged for me to start my researches in their country, and, in a way, opened the door for me. Singapore Airlines helped me to renew my acquaintance with their routes, and their London Office, particularly Mr. Tommy Kingston, provided many interesting details. K. L. M. too, through the good offices of Mr. John Turner-Lashmar, gave me wholehearted co-operation in my Indonesian research, and Qantas, British Airways and P. & O. willingly dug into their archives for historical detail. Gilbert Brown of Far East Travel Centre responded to incessant queries with tremendous patience and at speed; Kenneth Gould of Inchcapes supplied so much of his inexhaustible fund of knowledge on the whole area, particularly Singapore; Sheila Wong, Ng Sui On and Chris Quah in Penang aided and abetted with enthusiasm, as Kamala Gopi and Ong Beng Khim did in Singapore.

But, most of all, I would like to pay tribute to the Tourist Development Corporation of Malaysia and to the Singapore Tourist Promotion Board for the generous advice, help, opportunities, information and many personal kindnesses bestowed upon me during my recent visits, and lastly, but by no means least, Noelle Mostyn.

Introduction

I was on deck before dawn on the morning that I saw Malaysia for the first time. The sea slapped idly at the *Canton* as she moved landwards, and my nostrils, accustomed for three long weeks to the salty tang of the open sea, were assailed by rich earth odours drifting in the humid air, while the unfamiliar contours of Penang Island loomed like grey spectres in the lightening sky. Then, redfaced and angry at being disturbed, the sun arrived, transforming hillsides, forests and buildings with his reflected choler, while the sky turned slowly into morning azure. The quayside clattered into noisy activity, and, as the breeze died in the shelter of the harbour, a band of sweat formed at my waist, a sensation which was to become part and parcel of existence in the years that followed. Small knots of people were waiting on the dock, and, looming above one Chinese group, consisting of a man, woman and three small children, I saw the familiar bulk of my husband. The Chinese family were friends of his from Singapore who were visiting relations in Penang and had come in force to welcome me, and, since that first introduction, 20 years ago, I have never quite been able to divide Malaysia and Singapore neatly into separate entities as the politicians seem to do. So many of the people that I came to know during my sojourns in South-East Asia have relatives sprinkled liberally through the region, and come and go happily between them. In addition, the very proximity of the two nations and their ways of life, add to their similarities, while the intermingling of their history makes it necessary, when speaking or writing of one or the other, to refer back to past occurrences of mutual interest.

Nevertheless, there are very considerable contrasts, caused not only by the national traits of the predominant races in each place, and their longstanding rivalries, but also by the difference in size between the two, and the developments within them, which stretch even into present-day tourism. Such developments and rivalries are among the many fascinating aspects of any comment one makes on Malaysia and Singapore, for, although they argue furiously on occasion, neither can really afford to lose the other, and it is this almost 'Tom and Jerry' relationship which inevitably has effects far beyond their own confines and contains much of their inner strength. Loving them both, each for their own especial qualities, I can only wish them peace and prosperity in which to develop in harmonious disharmony along their separate, but inevitably united, paths.

Malaysia and Singapore embrace such a large area, not only physically but also historically, that it is not possible to cover everything in a book of this size; so I have concentrated mostly on areas and happenings that a tourist, or a business visitor with a few hours to spare, could discover for himself. I am deeply conscious that this will inevitably lead to some gaps in coverage, and I ask pardon of those lovely places and people that I have of necessity had to leave out. But the consolation must surely lie in the knowledge that there must always be something left for next time, which perhaps could also be considered to be one of the secrets of success in today's tourism scene.

Gladys Nicol

1. From Yesterday to Today

'Turn left at the bottom of Africa, past India and keep straight on. Sooner or later you'll come to the Malay States.' That might have been the directions given to the first explorers from the Northern Hemisphere who went in search of Peninsular Malaysia, the long, expressive, Eastern finger which points downward from Burma and Thailand towards Indonesia and Borneo. Singapore, joined to the Peninsula by the man-made Johore Causeway, is a protective nail on that finger, stopping within 85 miles of the equator. Although modern Malaysia also includes Sabah and Sarawak, two States in the great island of Borneo, this is a relatively recent happening, but it is quite logical if one is to think of Malaysia as a community mainly composed of Malay peoples. Yet it isn't quite as simple as that, for many different races have found their way over the centuries to this curving corner of South-East Asia, and one finds Chinese, Indians, Europeans, Malays and combinations of all of them, living more or less amicably together, each preserving their own ways and their own beliefs in a free and democratic society. We, in Europe, are still inclined to think of Singapore and Malaysia as comparatively 'new' nations, even though they are fully-fledged members of that melting pot of the world's hopes that we call the United Nations. Certainly they are older and wiser than some of the emergent African nations, but very young in comparison to the 'old hands' in the rest of the world. Yet it is likely that there were civilisations in the Malay Peninsula and the islands while we were still daubing paint on our faces, or when Attila ravaged his way across his known world. Granted the civilisations were different, but that some community life existed is beyond doubt. Some of them continue today in astonishingly pure and untouched forms in primitive tribes within the shadowed heart of Malaysia's jungles, as far removed from the modern city Malay as they are from the citizens of New York or London.

If we start in time-honoured fashion at the beginning, 'once upon a time' would seem to be as good a way as any, for the beginnings of Malaysia are shrouded in the mists of time, just as early sea mists hang like curtains around her rain-forests, among the oldest of their kind in the world. It is estimated that the great jungles remained inviolate for something like a 100 million years, and, while much of the world was gripped in the Ice Age, the myriad creatures which dwelt in the green steaminess of Malaysian forests remained undisturbed and relatively unchanged. As well as primitive man, therefore, many other creatures retained their original forms and can be found nowhere else in the world. In some ways this is not surprising, for – despite the concrete jungles of civilisation which insinuate themselves further into the green ones, tarmacadam roads and asphalt runways which replace old trails, tin mine scars, and rubber, palm oil, and rice plantations – two thirds of all Malaysia is still primeval forest and mangrove swamp, so that wildlife keeps a chance of survival; but, of course, how long this can continue is dependent on modern man and his demands.

Much is due to the hitherto sheer inaccessibility and difficulty of the hinterland terrain. Peninsular Malaysia, the original Malaya, for instance, covers approximately 5,000 square miles and boasts a coastline of over 1,000 miles. The central mountain ranges form a steep skullcap, rising to 7,000 feet at Gunong Tahan. On the western side, descent is steep, so that rivers rush headlong down the slopes in a pattern of waterfalls and fast-flowing streams, before reaching the 50-mile-wide coastal plain which faces Sumatra across the narrow Malaccan strait. On the eastern side of the range, the contours are more gradual, with longer, lazier rivers eventually flowing into the South China Sea across palm-lined beaches where there is little or no natural harbouring. Likewise, Sabah, covering about 29,388 square miles of the northern cap of Borneo, has mountain ranges which rise majestically all the way to the 13,455 feet of Kinabalu, highest mountain in South-East Asia. Three-quarters of the population live along the swampy coastal strips facing the South China Sea in the west, and the Sulu and Celebes Seas in the east. The dense tropical forests which cover the slopes have therefore been left to the aborigine tribes, and to the orang-utan ('forest man' in Malay) who has also dwelt there for thousands of years. Sarawak, with its romantic White Rajah image, and its fascinating little capital of Kuching, is a composition of mangrove swamp, wide rivers and virtually unexplored jungle, set against a backcloth of high mountains.

Singapore is a different story. Roughly the size of the Isle of Wight, and covering, together with 54 other small islands in the vicinity, a total area of about 225 square miles, its bursting population of two and a half million people, mostly of Chinese stock, has entailed the clearance and reclamation of most of its territory to accommodate them in housing and industrial developments. However, there too, one can find an area of about 12 square miles in the Bukit Panjang district which is marked off as a catchment and nature reserve, and there are traces of the original landscape, though little wildlife remains.

The predominantly unchanging quality of all these places is their climate, for their proximity to the equator ensures an eternal warmth and humidity. There is a considerable rainfall, as well as hot sunshine, throughout the year. In most parts, temperature changes vary only slightly between 75 and 87°F although in the higher areas, such as Cameron Highlands hill station in Peninsular Malaysia, temperatures have been recorded as low as 36°F. Seasons are indicated by a higher incidence of rainfall between October and January with the coming of the north-east Monsoon. This is usually followed by a drier spell between February and July, although, in common with many other places in the world, weather patterns have changed slightly in recent years. These seasonal changes are not immediately apparent to a newcomer from northern climes, for, when someone arrives by air in December, when London and Paris are cold and grey, the descent into the steamy heat provides great contrast even if skies are clouded, so that the spectacle of local people donning woolly cardigans is unbelievable. But, on longer acquaintance, the expatriate finds himself doing exactly the same thing, for when his own blood is thinned by tropical living he also immediately notices the sudden drop in temperature engendered by violent, sometimes prolonged rainstorms. These rainstorms come quite suddenly. It can be hot and sunny, and then the thunderheads start to build up. Skies darken to a blackish hue more in keeping with a northern December. The rain might last for anything from half an hour to several hours, then clear as the sun appears again. It is always cooler for a while, but then it becomes extremely humid. Nights are usually cool and pleasant and quite often one can sleep in comfort without air-conditioning, particularly if living near the coast, or in the hills. Inland, though, it is usually very warm at night as well.

It is this regular rainfall which accounts for the intense greenness. It is mostly the darkish green of tropical vegetation, but it is sharpened by paler shades, such as the exquisitely delicate hue of growing rice plantations, where the slender stems wave above the water, and it is also enlivened seasonally by the brilliance of flowers. The length and breadth of South-East Asia has a wealth of magnificent floral adornment, though, sadly, few of the blooms have perfume and even fewer, apart from orchids, blossom for more than a day or two. But they are so prolific that only a European, used to conserving his precious blooms, will grieve at the brevity of their life or even note the daily requirement to replenish flower vases, changing the water to prevent mosquitoes from breeding. Local people accept the flowers around them as part of life, sometimes using them for personal or general adornment, or as offerings at shrines, but, as in so many other facets of life in the East, the period of beauty is expected to be ephemeral.

Who are the Malaysians? What do they look like? Where did they come from? What language do they speak? The name gives a clue. Malay is a racial expression, referring to peoples of Malay stock, which ethnically nowadays means Muslim. The suffix '-sians' extends the word to include others such as Chinese, Indians and all the mixtures of races who have come to settle in the territories over the centuries. Mohammedanism reached the Peninsula in the thirteenth century with traders, and the Malay people embraced the religion universally some 200 years later. As far as today's Malaysians are concerned, it is difficult to lay down hard and fast rules on their looks, because the nation consists of so many different races and mixtures of colours and creeds. But one could divide them into the three races which comprise the majority of the Malaysian as well as the Singaporean peoples, on the understanding that, in addition, one will meet many who do not resemble any of the categories, or conversely could be mixtures of all of them. The main difficulty in attempting to categorise at all is the fact that within each race there are many tribal or provincial differences, dependent a great deal on the place of origin, even if that origin is centuries since. Occidentals are notoriously unable to distinguish between Malay, Chinese, Thai or even Japanese, let alone define the finer differences in facial and bodily structures between people who live in the same country, and particularly does this become difficult when many Straits- or Malaysian-born Chinese women (the nonyas) adopt Malay clothing, so that traditional Chinese attire of samfoo or cheongsam are not there to help identification. It might be easier to mention a similarity first for one example of this sticks in my mind. I was in the stands at Singapore Racecourse some years ago. The turf was brilliantly green, the racing perfect and the air remarkably mild. It could have been a very hot day at Ascot, until one looked at the preponderantly male crowd below. Their colouring could have been part of Cecil Beaton's designs for 'My Fair Lady', for all the hair was jet black and all the shirts white. If one sees light hair, there is undoubtedly European blood somewhere.

Malays are a most attractive people. Their colouring is anything from coffee to dark chocolate, with thick black hair, mostly straight, luminous dark eyes, high cheekbones and flattish short noses. When they smile, as they do very frequently, the teeth of the younger people are very white, though those of older generations are mostly marred by the constant use of betel. They aren't very tall, though the men are usually sturdy. Women, particularly when very young, are slender, often with exquisitely chiselled features, but many tend to round off a bit in later years. It is extremely difficult to assess age in both sexes, though I do find that on the whole men age less, particularly in country communities where womenfolk spend so much time in farm-labouring activities. They are a courteous, gentle, highly artistic people with a childlike sense of humour, who have the endearing, though sometimes infuriating, habit of never doing anything today if tomorrow will serve as well. I cannot ever remember seeing a Malay move at anything other than a slow pace, nor raise his voice above a whisper in normal conversation. They have been referred to as 'Nature's gentlemen'. The description cannot be bettered.

It is the West who have given the Chinese an identification as one race. The Chinese themselves didn't do it. A Hokkien is nothing like a Hakka. Hainanese cooking differs greatly from Pekinese, so that within Chinese communities there are very considerable variants, from the short, well-covered Cantonese, to the tall bony men from Shanghai. Not all are even yellow, for skin colouring varies from ivory to amber. About the only thing they have in common, that an outsider can easily recognise, is their universal tendency to smile at everything. And the smile can mean almost anything. I once had a Cantonese cook amah (nursemaid) who nearly caused me to commit mayhem when she dropped a precious piece of porcelain soon after I arrived in Singapore. It wasn't the loss of the item. It was the peals of laughter she emitted. From behind her hand. I soon learned though, for she'd laugh at children's antics in the same shrill way, but without the hand; at family good news with nods of her sleek black head; stood firmly and meaningly to attention while listening to the radio on Christmas Day for 'Missie Queen' while gleaming smiles came from her gold teeth, and, when we said goodbye for the last time, she laughed again, but then, there were tears in her eyes as well as in mine. . . . Most Chinese are more go-ahead, more impatient, louder-voiced than their Malay compatriots and it is no wonder that their tremendous flair for business activities have made them so rich and powerful in Malaysia and in Singapore. A greatly respected and well-known Chinese millionaire, now alas with his ancestors, once commented to my husband just before the advent of Singapore's independence when Malayanisation of all jobs was the order of the day. 'It is a pity that so many of you are going home. You should stay and work in Government with us. That is what you British are so very good at. Then we go on with the moneymaking. That is what we do best. We make a fine team.' He was a highly perceptive man, so his comment was probably accurate.

There is no difficulty in identifying the Indians among the Malaysian and Singaporean communities, particularly for Britons long used to so many of them living in our midst in the U.K., although they too vary greatly among themselves. With the exception of the light-skinned Parsees, their skins are usually darker than either Malays or Chinese, noses are longer and higher bridged, and they are usually taller. Tourists to Malaysia and Singapore will meet Indians mostly in tailoring, curio and haberdashery emporiums as well as working as doormen, drivers, nightwatchmen, etc. The Indian woman comes into her own in the tropical warmth. Her graceful sari is no longer marred by thick cardigans, or her pretty sandals stretched with woolly socks. She regains her natural dignity and the transformation, from the chrysalis murk of British winter, is a joy to behold, particularly for the first time. All the Asian women have one thing in common. On festive occasions, they appear, brilliant as butterflies in fine gauzes and silks, so that every European woman, whatever her age, and even if wearing the latest Dior creation, feels exactly like an overdressed elephant.

With so many tongues, Chinese, Malay, Tamil and all the dialects of each, how can they communicate? Malay is now the national tongue both in Malaysia and Singapore and most people understand this. But in addition, English is still widely used after the long years of British influence, particularly in law and in government, and there seems no inclination to change this state of affairs. There are schools in each language including English, for even anti-British elements realise that the ability to read and speak English is a built-in asset in communicating with the rest of the world. Other world languages are taught too, and it is not uncommon to find well educated Malaysians or Singaporeans speaking eight or nine languages, not counting dialects. In tourism, there are multi-lingual guides and the number grows yearly as the need to understand people from all over the world grows too.

Where do the Malays come from? Opinions from anthropologists and archaeologists incline to the theories that the earliest men in South-East Asia were probably those who lived in the limestone caves in Borneo and the Peninsula, and whose strange wall-paintings still survive in the Niah Caves. As we have seen, the area was untouched by the Ice Age, and the early men lived on using crude stone axes to carve their existence. In the Peninsula, the aborigine tribes who call themselves Orang Asli ('original man' in Malay) stem directly in their ancestry through a period of about seven thousand years, and they encompass various early migrations which came down from Yunan and which spread right into the Indonesian islands. Certainly many Malays have an almost Chinese appearance. These tribes were mainly cave-dwellers, but they had learned to master fire, and although they still used the primitive stone weapons, they could cook their food. But when they tried to move out of the jungles towards the sea, they were driven back by the Proto-Malays, their slightly more sophisticated cousins who, by about 2000 B.C. were using metal tools and had taken up positions as fishermen along the coasts. But the move seawards could hardly have been a conscious search for new areas, for even today the Orang Asli live in their close-knit groups or tribes, retaining their own religions, language and life-patterns. It is only very recently that they have started to dwell in clearings on the edge of the jungles as well as deep within them. You can visit one of these on the road from Kuala Lumpur to Bentong.

With a department of Orang Asli affairs within the Malaysian Government it can only be a matter of a generation or two before they are drawn into modern Malay society, rather than the decades it has taken to come this far. One hopes that they will not lose all their identity in the achievement of this pattern, for then the last links with the Malaysian Stone Age would be lost forever.

Apart from these aboriginal peoples, the origin of the Malay is somewhat unclear, but it is believed that ancestors of the present race came from southern India into Sumatra, intermarried with the locals and spread from there into Java, Singapore, Borneo, the Malay Peninsula, etc. There is an area called Mallia in southern India which would give credence to this theory. There is, in addition, an ancient book, known as the Malay Annals, which has very many truths hidden within its tall stories and legends, and it says that Bukit Siguntang Maha Meru (Gunong Dempo) in the State of Palembang in Sumatra, is the place of origin of the Malay. There is a river there called Sungei Malayu, which could have given its name to the area and to the people living nearby, calling themselves Orang Malayu. We can also see that many places in Malaysia have Indian names, and Sir Frank Swettenham is on record as saying that, in his day, when Malays in Perak reverted to old superstitions to invoke evil spirits, they used an incomprehensible incantation which could be linked to Sanskrit.

In the year 160 A.D., the name Malaya appeared on the maps of the ancient Greek world for the first time. The words spelled out Golden Chersonese, and were put there by Ptolemy. Because of this link, one is inclined to believe that there may be some truth in the claim, put forward by a Raja Bachitram Shah, known later as Sang Seperba, around the beginning of the twelfth century, that he was a direct descendant of Alexander the Great. (How this fits into the story you will see but don't lose sight of it.) Of course, the coasts of Malaysia had been well known to sailors who brought the trading junks across the China Sea and into the Indian Ocean via the Straits of Malacca for many centuries before that. They must have been fearsome journeys for the little ships of

the times, braving unknown waters and facing the twin
hazards of monsoon storms and the depredations of the
pirates who lay in wait for them. A man called Fa-Hsien,
writing in 414 A.D. has left us a graphic description of the
scene on a journey between Sumatra and China. . . . 'In the
darkness of the night, only great waves were to be seen, breaking on one another and emitting a brightness like that of fire,
with large turtles and other monsters of the deep all about'.
. . . Today's travellers in the region still marvel at the
phosphorescence which plays about the sides of their larger
vessels, and my own first journey through the Straits had
something of a similar feeling. I can vividly recall the eerie,
shining lights on the sea, and the sickening fascination as the
liner ploughed through vast, glutinous masses of Portuguese
men o' war. Mr. Fa-Hsien must have been much nearer to
sea-level in his craft, and the 'monsters' must have looked an
awful lot bigger to him.

Certainly we know that before the birth of Christ, traders
from the Coromandel coast of India came to the East, looking
for ivory, sandalwood, camphor, tin and the precious spices.
For a long while, they used to anchor on the west coast of
Malaya in the area we call the Kra Isthmus, and then employ
bearers to carry the cargoes over the mountains to re-embark
in other ships on the eastern seaboard. But probably because
of the sheer inconvenience and difficulties of obtaining sufficient ships, they forged on down through the Straits and all
the way around the coasts, past the then uninhabited island
we now call Singapore, and trading settlements appeared at
the mouths of rivers to supply ships with fresh fruit and water
so necessary to healthy survival. It was inevitable of course
that some of the more weary voyagers should go no further. In
addition merchants lingered, foreseeing the immense riches
which would be theirs as middlemen on the Spice Route. By
200 A.D. when gold had been found in Malaya's red earth,
they were joined by adventurers from all over the known
world. Even the Romans found their way to the Golden Chersonese, but it was the Indians who came in greatest numbers,
bringing the Hindu religion with them and marrying into

local families, so that, within several generations, 'River States' had sprung up at the estuaries. The rulers lived in great splendour, for according to Hindu beliefs, kings were divine, so that each was in effect a despot, seldom seen by his subjects except when he journeyed forth from his double-gated walled town in a white howdah on the back of an elephant. The ancient lineage of the Malay rulers comes from this period.

It was only just before World War Two that an archaeologist discovered temples and houses which could definitely be dated between the 5th and 12th centuries on a site known in Hindu Sanskrit as Kataha. It lies in the shadow of Jerai Mountain, visible to every ship plying the Straits of Malacca. The name, when translated into modern Malay, is Kedah. As the ruling house of Kedah is a particularly interesting and important one in the light of contemporary history, I propose to go a little deeper into its background, but I would point out that all the royal houses have had their own fascinating parts to play in the moulding of present day Malaysia, and each would fill a chapter on its own.

The Kedah dynasty has been in existence for over a thousand years, from the time when a Mongol prince, Marong Mahawongsa, was on his way to China to marry a Mongol princess. His ship was wrecked in the storms which beset the Straits, and he landed with other survivors. Fortunately for him, the local populace took a fancy to him and made him Ruler, and, since that time, there have been nine Hindu rulers and sixteen Muslim ones in direct line. (Mohammedanism became the religion of Malaysia in the fifteenth century, which explains the changeover.)

During the sixteenth century, Kedah traded with the port of Malacca, some distance to the south of the Peninsula, and with China. But with the advent of the Dutch in the seventeenth century, who placed trading restrictions on ports under their jurisdiction, Kedah transferred its affections across the Bay of Bengal to an English trading company in Calcutta, which had received its charter from Queen Elizabeth the First on the last day of December 1599, and was none other than the East India Company. Among its archives, there is a reference to the possibility of the sale of 'tin from Queda', so one sees that the first association of the East India Company with Peninsular Malaya came through Kedah. This in its turn brought the ships of the Company to the mouth of the Kedah River to set up a trading post, known then as a 'factory'.

In 1700, an Alexander Hamilton wrote a description of the Sultan of Kedah, which said . . . 'he never failes of visiting stranger merchants at their coming to his port, and then, according to Custom, he must have a present. When the stranger returns the visit, or has any business with him, he must make him a present, otherwise he thinks due respect is not paid to him.' After this exchange of presents and visits, Hamilton says, 'His Majesty will honour the Stranger with a seat near his sacred person and will chew a little Betel and put it out of his Royal Mouth on to a little gold saucer and sends it by his page to the Stranger, who must take it with all the signs of humility and satisfaction and chew it after him, and it is very dangerous to refuse the Royal Morsel . . .'!

By 1765, there was a young man called Francis Light trading in Kedah. He wrote to his company saying that the Ruler wished to grant them the seaport of Kedah in return for assistance against his enemies, the Bugis, and the very greatly feared and powerful Siamese. There had been some interest shown by Warren Hastings in the scheme, but England had been engaged in one of her interminable wars with France, and nothing concrete happened until 1786, when Light, acting on behalf of the Governor-General in Calcutta, signed a treaty with Sultan Abdullah the Second. In 1791, another treaty was signed between Kedah and the British which allowed the Sultan 6000 Spanish dollars per annum, so long as the British occupied Penang, or Prince of Wales Island as they called it. In 1800 Abdullah's successor agreed to part with a strip of land on the mainland opposite Penang Island for a further 4000 dollars per annum, and the area was renamed Province Wellesley. According to records, the original arrangements in 1786 had been tacitly agreed and understood by Sultan Abdullah to include military assistance, but no mention was made in later agreements, and when, in 1821, the Siamese actually made the long-feared attack and overran Kedah, putting the population to the sword, the British took no part in the proceedings apart from giving hospitality to the Sultan when he fled from Kedah. 'This breach of faith', says Sir Frank Swettenham in his fascinating book *British Malaya*, 'sullied the British name and weakened its influence with Malays for very many years.' The Sultan died in exile, his favourite son was taken to Siam as hostage, his principal minister was captured and, it is believed, poisoned, and it was not until 1842 that the sultanate operated again. In the meantime, Siam had thrust into Perak with some victory, and had thoughts about attacking Selangor, but that attack never materialised, and with an Anglo/Siamese agreement in 1826, the Siamese returned to Ligor in southern Siam.

In the light of all this, it is revealing that, in 1894, Sultan Abdul Hamid Halim Shar prevailed upon the Siamese Government to allow the appointment of a British consul in his State. In 1909 he signed the Anglo-Kedah treaty which brought his State directly, into the sphere of British influence. When in August 1957 the Declaration of Independence was read in Kuala Lumpur by the first Prime Minister of the Federation of Malaya, the voice was that of Tunku Abdul Rahman Putre Al-Haj, fourth son of the Siamese sixth wife of the Sultan of Kedah. So does history turn full circle.

It was during the thirteenth century that the Siamese had first come southwards to overrun and conquer the northern Malay States of Kelantan, Trengganu and Kedah, and until the twentieth century had remained as big brother, so there is a considerable injection of Siamese blood into these areas, often seen in local facial structures. Apart from these more homely asides, the acquirement of a kind of overlord had been rather an expensive one for the Malays, for the Siamese extracted tribute every three years, and it had to be in gold or silver. But it took a far more artistic form than mere bars or coin. It was modelled into stylised trees with birds, snakes and flowers entwined into the branches, and its Malay name was

Bungah Emas, meaning the gold flowers. There was a nice line in distinction between the interpretation put upon the tributes by Siam and the Malay States. The Siamese said the golden flowers were the sign of submission by a vassal. The Malays called them gifts, but paid them just the same. There is a description of one of these trees, sent to Bangkok in 1869 by the Ruler of Kelantan. It says that it had eight branches, thirty-eight flowers, nine hundred and eight leaves, four snakes and four pairs of birds, all worked in gold. A gift indeed. . . . When I was in Bangkok recently, I thought it might be interesting to try and see one of these trees. After some enquiry, I discovered that, in fact the trees do still exist, and are in the Royal Treasury, safely locked up in the vaults. I was therefore unable to see them, or the replicas which are apparently in rooms in the Royal Palace, but, in the Coronation Room, on either side of the throne, there are some of these stylised trees also in replica, so one is able to get a fair idea of their form, which is rather different to the attractive little silver- and gold-leaved trees seen in all the Thai temples. The stylised ones look more like umbrella- and hat-stands, and I found them just a little disappointing. But remembering that the originals were in solid gold and silver, who was I to criticise?

There is one more interesting point before we leave the Bungah Emas. When the Anglo-Kedah treaty was signed in 1909, the golden flowers were already prepared for presentation to the King of Siam. Instead, they were sent to King Edward Seventh in London. They were the last of a very long line.

You will remember that I mentioned a certain Sang Seperba. It is said that he had arrived in Palembang in Sumatra, found favour with the local chief, married his daughter, and in time became the ruler. Then, he had sailed on to Bentan, where he spread his favours sufficiently to acquire another son, named Sang Nila Utama, before journeying back to yet another state in Sumatra, called Menangkabau. Sang Nila Utama, true to family tradition, married the daughter of the ruler before he left Bentan to settle on a neighbouring island. Writing in 1848, a Mr. J. R. Logan proposed the interesting theory that he married the daughter of the chief of the new island before becoming *its* ruler in 1160. I think it highly likely that he did both, but the point is that this new island was known as Tamasek, an Indian name, meaning a place of festivals, although I have also seen its meaning given as 'port'. Legend says that Sang Nila Utama renamed the place Singapure, city of the Lion, because he had seen an animal near the site of his new city which he described as 'very swift and beautiful, its body bright red, its head jet black, its breast white, in size larger than a he-goat'. With a story like that to support its name is it any less likely that it was indeed the descendant of Alexander the Great who founded the ancient city of Singapure, upon whose site, centuries later, the present great city of Singapore was to be built?

Sang Nila Utama died in 1209, and was succeeded by his descendants who in their turn helped the city to prosper, and in so doing attracted the jealousy of the Raja of Majapahit in Java. He sent an expedition to attack Singapure, but it was beaten off with some losses. However, in about the year 1252, the Ruler of Singapura, Iskander by name (is this derived from Alexander?) killed off one of his wives for some offence. The execution, by impaling, took place in public, and the lady's father, Sang Ranjuna Tapa, who was the Prime Minister (Bendahara) at that time, was so enraged, either by the execution or the method of it, that he told the Javanese Raja of Majapahit to try again, and, that this time, he would arrange that the gates of the city were left open for him. The Javanese came in the night, entered the city and put most of the inhabitants to death. But a few escaped. They crossed the narrow strait which divided the island city from the mainland, and wandered northwards for a long time. They founded a new city at Malacca, where they and their descendants lived at peace until the Portuguese came. Another version of the story says that it was perhaps poetic justice that Majapahit himself was pushed out of Singapura by the Siamese who set up a governorship. This too was replaced, none too gently, by a Majapahit prince called Parameswara who then became a pirate, the main occupation of the time. Again the Siamese came south, put the prince to flight and destroyed the city. It was to sleep under the jungle for several hundred years until Raffles' kiss wakened it back into the history books.

Sejaru Melayu, the earliest Malay history which records most of these events, also dwells on the fate of the Bendahara who had been responsible for the downfall of Singapure. It says . . . 'By the power of God Almighty, the house of Sang Ranjuna Tapa became a ruin, its pillars fell and rice was no longer planted. And Sang Ranjuna Tapa together with his wife, were changed into stones and these are the stones which may be seen lying by the river of Singapura.' Sir Frank Swettenham writes that early in the last century there had indeed been a strange stone lying by the Singapore river which had an undecipherable inscription. It was blown to bits by vandals, and although some fragments were sent to the Calcutta Museum where, for all that I can ascertain, they still seem to be, the rest of the stone was used as 'fill' on the swamp on which the new town was built. So when walking in the very small part of old Singapore which remains today, perhaps along Boat Quay, or Fullerton Square and the vicinity, which were part of the original city, one treads a long long way back into the uncertain past. . . . It is, at least, a nice theory.

In the yellowed pages of earlier times, it is the name of Malacca which appears most frequently, mainly because its geographical position on the west coast of the Peninsula made it a most convenient stopping place on East/West trade routes. The date of arrival of the refugees from Tamasek is popularly placed at the opening of the fifteenth century, and the name of the ruler is given as Parameswara. It was soon after this that the Chinese Admiral Cheng Ho arrived in the port, bringing compliments and gifts from his master the Emperor of China, Son of Heaven. Parameswara returned the visit and was proclaimed by the Emperor as King of Malacca and the mountains beyond. One of the customs he brought back with him from that sortie was a yellow umbrella as the sign of his royalty, still part of the panoply of the rulers in

Malaysia. It is also from around this time that we begin to find references to Islam, for before Parameswara died he had been converted to that faith. There were already many settlers from the Near and Middle East in Malacca, and there must have been a considerable number of Mohammedans among them. In 1503, Lewis Wertemans of Rome comments, 'When we came to the city of Malacka which some call Meleka, we were incontinent commanded to come to the Sultan being a Mahomedan and subject to the Great Sultan of China and payeth him tribute of which the cause is that more than eighty years ago that city was builded by the Sultan of China for none other cause than only for the commodity of the haven, being doubtless one of the fairest in that ocean.'

I have already commented that the Malays were a civilised people in early times. In Stanley's translation of the manuscript attributed to Duarte Barbose, there is a very full description of the Malays in the beginning of the sixteenth century. (Incidentally, Mr. Stanley considered that this description was really the work of Magellan.) It says,

'This city of Malaca is the richest trading port and possesses the most valuable merchandise, and most numerous shipping and extensive traffic that is known in all the world. And it has got such a quantity of gold that the great merchants do not estimate their property nor reckon otherwise than by bahars of gold which are four quintals each bahar (400lbs = one bahar). There are merchants among them who will take up singly three or four ships laden with very valuable goods and will supply them with cargo from their own property. They are very well made men and likewise the women. They are of a brown colour and go bare from the waist upwards and from that downwards cover themselves with silk and cotton cloths and they wear short jackets halfway down the thigh of scarlet cloth and silk cotton or brocade stuffs and they are girt with belts and carry daggers in their waists wrought with rich inlaid work. And the women dress in wraps of silk stuffs and short skirts much adorned with gold and jewellery and have long beautiful hair. These people have many mosques and when they die they bury their bodies. Their children inherit from them. They live in large houses and have gardens and orchards and pools of water outside the city for their recreation. They have got many slaves who are married with wives and children. These slaves live separately and serve them when they have need of them. These Moors who are named Malays are very polished people and gentlemen." Not unnaturally the fame of Malacca spread. 'Whoever is Lord of Malacca' wrote a Portuguese of the time, 'has his hands on the throat of Venice.' His countrymen agreed, for they wanted to snatch the monopoly of the valuable spice trade from the Venetian merchants and in 1511, Albuquerque and his soldiers stormed the city. Elephants and bravery were no match for gunpowder, and the Portuguese won the day. Almost immediately, they started to build a fortress, whose few remnants may still be seen. They also made it a policy to infuse Portuguese blood into the community by marrying into local families and it is from this time that the strong Eurasian elements start to appear in Malaya. The Eurasians who live in their own separate estate in Malacca speak Cristao, a Portuguese dialect which has been remarked as pure sixteenth-century speech. During the nineteenth century, the Royal library in Brussels yielded a manuscript written by a Manuel Godinho de Eredia in 1613, and addressed to Philippe the Third of Spain. Godinho de Eredia was born in Malacca in 1563, the son of a Portuguese nobleman and a Malay princess, and he claimed that the name Malacca came from a tree of that name. He said also that in 1600 the remains of the tomb of the founder were to be seen on the rocky promontory called Tanjong Tuan. The headland naturally remains, but there is no sign of the tomb. But, in direct translation, its name means Master's promontory. The Portuguese remained in Malacca for 130 years before the Dutch invaded in 1641 and drove them out. In usual thorough Dutch fashion they tidied the place up a bit and made it their headquarters. From there, they opened stations in Perak, Selangor and elsewhere, trading for tin. And they continued to possess Malacca until 1795, when it was first captured by the British.

There is an interesting echo of Malaysia far across the sea in South Africa, also full of historical influences of the Portuguese and Dutch. The discovery by Vasco da Gama of the Cape Route to the Spice Islands had provided a valuable refuelling and victualling stop on the long hard journey. The Dutch required people to work the gardens of fruit and vegetables and as, under Dutch laws, aboriginal peoples could not be made into slaves, they imported a number of Malay slaves to do the work. Slavery was abolished in 1833, but by that time Malays had become part of the Cape population, keeping their Moslem religion. In one small area of mushrooming Cape Town, there are still remnants of what has always been known as 'The Malay Quarter'.

In 1781, during the American War of Independence, a boy was born to the wife of the Captain, on board the West Indiaman *Ann*, a ship in one of the convoys. His influence upon Malaysia and Singapore in later years was to be among the most far-reaching of all Europeans. Thomas Stamford Bingley Raffles was one of six children, and, due to the penurious circumstances in which the family lived, he was placed in a temporary position as a clerk in the offices of the East India Company, at the tender age of fourteen, after a lamentably sketchy education of two years. During the ten years which followed, he worked during the day, and educated himself at night, until, in 1805, he was sent to the Penang Office as assistant secretary to the Governor. Just prior to this posting he had married Olivia Fancourt, the widow of a surgeon who had died in Madras. They left England in April 1805 and on the six-month journey to Penang, Raffles learned to speak Malay in readiness for his appointment. It was due to this application to study that he was able, almost immediately on arrival in his new post, to strike an affinity with the Malays, learning about their living conditions, history, religious customs, etc., a knowledge which was to turn him into one of the greatest experts of his time on East Asian affairs and which also brought him to the notice of Lord Minto, the then Governor-General of India. The Napoleonic wars were in full spate in Europe and Napoleon's brother was sitting on the Dutch throne. When in

1807 he sent a Governor-General to take over Dutch colonies in the East Indies, Lord Minto realised that Raffles' unique knowledge of the Malay people could be turned to good account. He sent for the young man to come to Calcutta, created him Agent to the Governor-General and sent him back to the Straits with instructions to collect all the information necessary to facilitate a successful expeditionary force to Java. On 11th June 1811, a large force embarked from Malacca, under the direction of Lord Minto, for Batavia, and Raffles sailed with them as Chief Intelligence Officer. The sortie was highly successful and, within six weeks, Raffles was installed as Lieutenant-Governor of Java. Minto returned to Calcutta and a medal was struck in England to comemmorate the event. A very significant meeting occurred in Malacca as the result of the decision to use that town as embarkation point for the expeditionary forces. This was between Stamford Raffles and Abdullah, son of Abdulkadir, a fifteen-year-old Malay boy who worked in the office of Colonel Farquhar, then Resident and Commandant of Malacca. Raffles took a liking to the boy, employed him as a scribe, and many years later, inspired him to write Hikiaat Abdullah – Abdullah's history – which has provided many invaluable glimpses of life in his time. But the most important part of the writings he left us are the minutely detailed and graphic descriptions of Raffles himself which show us the man, and not just the founder of Singapore. There is, sadly, little room for quoting them here, but for those who are interested in knowing more than a cursory glimpse of history's events, I would highly recommend delving into the past through his words.

The next three years were busy ones for Raffles, who, despite bouts of fever and overwork, set about reforming Java's economies, banning the import of slaves and the use of torture, reorganising the judiciary system and even planning the restoration of Borobadur. But Waterloo, and the defeat of Napoleon in 1814, was to change the picture yet again. Holland, and the lands which now comprise modern Belgium, were to become part of an insurance against the repetition of French militarism as portrayed by Napoleon. South Africa's

Cape of Good Hope and the lovely island of Ceylon stayed under British rule, but Java and Malacca were to go back to Holland as demonstration of good intent, thus effectively putting the Straits back under Dutch control. In vain Raffles protested and in 1816 he left Java to return to England. But Olivia was not with him. She had died in 1814 and was buried in Java. The memorial to her can be seen in the Botanical Gardens at Bogor just outside Jakarta. It is a simple stone, set under a white pagoda, a reminder of only one of hundreds of women and children whose bones lay far from the country whose greatness they helped to build, just by their presence beside their menfolk.

We are told that Raffles campaigned furiously in England to rouse his hearers to 'defend our interest in the Eastern Archipelago, not only against the Dutch, but also against the Russians and the Americans' . . . familiar words, I feel. We are also told that his pleas fell on deaf ears but that he was given a knighthood and posted to Bencoolen in Sumatra as Governor-General. It is not the only time that such methods have been used to get rid of inconvenient importunists. He sailed in November 1817, with his new wife Sophia, and by the time the ship arrived in Sumatra in April 1818 she had given birth to a daughter. Again Raffles plunged into the job of putting order into his domain, which he once described as 'wretched, miserable and poor', but, at the same time, he wrote interminable letters to the Marquis of Hastings, who had become Governor-General of India. Eventually, Hastings suggested that Raffles came to see him, and once more the visionary embarked for Calcutta in 1818. He left there with official terms of reference to 'look for the establishment of a station beyond Malacca such as may command the Southern entrance of those Straits . . . and then . . . not the extension of any territorial influence, but strictly limited to the occupation of an advantageous position for the protection of our commerce.'

There is no doubt that the vast amount of information that Raffles had assimilated must have included a good deal about Tamasek or Singapura, which had been an important base for the great empire of Sri Vijaya, and from which it had been able to control the narrow seas between the South China Sea and the Indian Ocean. He must have kept the site well to the fore of his mind when attempting to fulfil Hastings' commission, despite instructions that he must thoroughly inspect Rhio and the fact that he also looked very closely at Siak and the Carimun Islands, much nearer to Sumatra, for on 12th December 1818, he wrote to his friend Marsden from the *Nearchus* . . . 'We are now on our way to the Eastward in the hope of doing something, but I must fear the Dutch have hardly left us an inch of ground to stand upon. My attention is principally turned to Johore, and you must not be surprised if my next letter to you is dated from the site of the ancient city of Singapura.'

Seven ships, *Nearchus, Margaret* and *Frances* (also known as *Discovery*), *Investigator, Ganges, Enterprise, Indiana* and *Mercury*, anchored off Singapore Island on the landward side of St. John's Island in the waters we know now as 'the Roads' on 28th January 1819. With Raffles, as he stepped ashore was Colonel Farquhar, Resident of Malacca, very well known and respected by the Malays. There remains one eye-witness description of the arrival. It is that of a Malay, We Hakim, who was fifteen at the time. . . . 'At the time when Raffles came there were under one hundred small houses and huts at the mouth of the river, but the Raja's house was the only large one . . . about half the Orang Laut (sea people) lived ashore and half in boats. . . . The men that lived in boats were the first to see Tuan Raffles coming . . . there were two white men and a Sepoy . . . when they landed they went straight to the Temenggong's house. Tuan Raffles was there. He was a short man. I knew his appearance. Tuan Farquhar was there. He was taller than Tuan Raffles and he wore a helmet. The sepoy carried a musket. They were entertained by the Temenggong and he gave them rambutans and all kinds of fruit. . . . Tuan Raffles went into the centre of the house. About four o'clock in the afternoon they came out and went on board again. . . .' A member of the expedition, John Crawford, wrote of the interview in the house, 'whatever the inmost sentiments of the

Malays' hearts may have been, they received Sir Stamford with great cordiality and friendship, declaring that nothing could give them greater happiness than to be in alliance with the English, but stated that it did not rest with them but with higher authority, the Rajahs of Rhio and Lingen, who were the Sovereigns of this country. . . .' Buckpassing is not, apparently, an entirely Western or modern innovation. . . .

The Rajahs were brothers. The younger had been proclaimed Viceroy and had Dutch sympathies. The other, Tunku Long, or Husein, was sent for by Raffles and proclaimed Sultan of Johore and recognised on behalf of the East India Company. A preliminary treaty had been concluded with the Temenggong of Johore on 30th January 1819, but on 6th February 1819, a new treaty was made between Raffles and Sultan Husein and the Temenggong, by which the Malays granted the British Government the right to settle on the island. Raffles himself left Singapore on 7th February 1819 in the *Indiana*, nine days from his arrival, leaving Farquhar in charge, but with explicit instruction on procedure.

The position was by no means secure. Protests were inevitable, the East India Board was furious and ministers of the Crown 'excessively angry'. But Raffles had effected a *fait accompli* and when businessmen began to take a healthy interest in the infant town, setting up their trading posts, protest died away in the face of monetary gain. Over the next two years, Raffles visited Singapore again from his post at Bencoolen where, incidentally, three of his children died from the fevers prevalent at the time. On his visits to 'his' City, he threw himself into various schemes for its future and these included three major projects which have had a lasting effect. These were, the Botanical Gardens, the Raffles Institute and the major portion of town planning. From the day he set foot in Singapore in January 1819 until he finally departed in June 1823, he had only actually lived in Singapore for nine months in all, but such was his influence and impact in this brief period that, despite all the sterling work accomplished by those Britons who followed after him, it is his name which is indissolubly linked with Singapore for all time. On 2nd

February, 1824, Raffles, his wife and one child, embarked from Bencoolen in a ship called *Fame* for England. With him he took his precious manuscripts, painstakingly prepared over the years on every detail of life, flora and fauna in Sumatra and Singapore. That very night, the ship caught fire, and though the little family escaped in a small boat, the manuscrips were destroyed, an untold loss to we who come later.

Two years later, broken in health and dunned by creditors, Raffles died, at the early age of forty-six. For many years, no-one knew where he was buried, until, quite by chance, his tomb was discovered in St. Mary's Church, Hendon, where he still lies, a far, far cry from the lands to which he had devoted almost all of his working life.

It was, in a way, through Raffles that Sarawak in Borneo eventually acquired a White Rajah. The young, elegant James Brooke was a great admirer of Sir Stamford Raffles and, because of that, made his way to the Far East, and eventually, in the *Royalist*, found his way up the curving ochre waters of the Sarawak River to quell a rising in 1839. For his extremely able handling of the situation he was asked by the local ruling classes to stay and become their Rajah ... the first of the White Rajahs of Sarawak. Sarawak, together with Sabah, formerly British North Borneo, together cover an area larger than all Peninsular Malaysia, but are, because of their geography, far less accessible than the Peninsula. However, they offer a visitor so much that is sheer exoticism that they must have room to themselves in this book. But it must never be forgotten that Chinese, as well as Britons, found their way to Borneo in days long past and have writ their names deep in her history, along with the tribes who were there before the history began. But I digress a little from the tracing of the main path. . . .

By 1825, the European see-saw had taken another tilt, and Malacca was once more under the British flag. In the years that followed, the ports and settlements along the western coast of Peninsula Malaysia, along with Singapore, were steadily prospering and, in 1867, they all became incorporated into the Crown Colony of the Straits Settlements. In these years it had also been the declared policy of the British Government not to interfere in the affairs of the Malay States, and impatient traders in Singapore and Penang were told that if they wanted to trade with the interior of the country they would do so at their own risk. But the presence of the British might was undoubtedly a deterrent to the pirates, Achinese, Bugis and even the powerful Siamese, and the Malay States were, in consequence, able to get on with the business of everyday living without constant threat of war. The States also prospered, Indians and Chinese came in vast numbers to work the tin mines in Perak, Selangor and Negri Sembilan, and Malay territorial chiefs grew in wealth from the tin they produced. Malays also spread inland from their concentrated communities at river mouths, to open up the land for agriculture. But the Sultans were weakened and divided within their own lands, and insurrection and anarchy were the order of the day. So serious did this become that the then Secretary of State for the Colonies, Lord Kimberley, wrote to Sir Andrew Clarke on his appointment as Governor of the Straits Settlements in the following terms on 20th September 1873. . . .'Her Majesty's Government have, it need hardly be said, no desire to interfere in the internal affairs of the Malay States. But looking to the long and intimate connection between them and the British Government and to the well-being of the British Settlements themselves, Her Majesty's Government find it incumbent upon them to employ such influence as they possess with the Native Princes to rescue if possible, those fertile and productive countries from the ruin which must befall them if the present disorders continue unchecked,' and then, further on, 'I should wish you especially to consider whether it would be advisable to appoint a British Officer to reside in any of the States. Such an appointment could of course, only be made with the full consent of the Native Government and the expenses connected with it would have to be defrayed by the Government of the Straits Settlements.'

The Treaty of Pangkor was accordingly signed on 20th January 1874 with Perak, Selangor and Sungei Ujong, followed in 1888 by Pahang (the other Malay States did not follow suit until well beyond the turn of the present century). It must not be thought that all this took place without a deal of troubles, for the Malay States were almost feudal, and peace-making was a new experience. In one particular incident a British resident Mr. J. W. W. Birch, was assassinated when feelings ran high. Eventually, the culprits were caught and condemned, not only by the British Authority, but by the Rulers, for it was considered that the hot-heads had taken it upon themselves to murder a man who was the guest of their country and were therefore guilty of treason against their Sultan. But on the whole, there was reason and understanding on both sides, and though mistakes occurred, there was considerable progress. Gradually the residents took more and more responsibility in introducing modern ways to the Protectorates to bring them from the feudal state, but they never in any way interfered in matters of religion and custom. In 1895, the First Federation took place between four States, with a central government in Kuala Lumpur. The other five states continued to develop along their own paths, and it was not until 1910 that Kedah, Kelantan, Trengganu and Perlis signed treaties with Britain and accepted British Advisers at their Courts. Johore followed in 1914, under a Treaty signed with Sultan Sir Ibrahim, but it had already been the most advanced State in the Peninsula. Under an earlier Sultan, Abu Bakar, who had travelled exten-sively in Europe and had been to England to meet Queen Vic-toria, the State had received a written Constitution. After the treaties were signed, British engineers, doctors, civil servants and others were sent out to help and advise wherever required, but the State Governments in Johore Bahru, Alor Star, Kota Bahru, Kuala Trengganu and Kangar dealt with the British High Commissioner through a Singapore Secretariat. It is very important to make it quite clear to those who were un-familiar with Malaysia that there was always a great difference between the Straits Settlements of Penang, Malacca and Singapore, and the Malay States. The latter were not British territory. There was always strong nationalism in the

States, particularly in Johore and in Kedah, and this eventually became a political force of great importance. One cannot pass over the years of Resident Advisers, however, without stressing the tremendous economic growth which took place. Much of this was due to easier accessibility from Europe with the opening of the Suez Canal in 1869. There was also the introduction of the railway. The first stretch ran from Taiping to Port Weld, a distance of eight miles. Completed in 1884, its construction was undertaken by two divisions of Ceylonese Pioneers. The next stretch was for 22 miles, between Kuala Lumpur and Klang, vital for the booming trade links, but none of this work was accomplished without heavy loss of life mostly from malaria. In Calcutta, Sir Donald Ross had discovered that malaria was carried by a mosquito, but it was a doctor, working on an estate in Klang who started to campaign for clearance of the swamps and streams in an effort to stop the mosquitoes from breeding. Dr. Malcom Watson later received a knighthood for his work for, thanks to him, towns and estates were freed from the dreaded pest for the first time. Malaya, therefore, was the first tropical country to take advantage of Sir Donald Ross's discoveries, and this was probably her greatest achievement for mankind.

World War One brushed lightly over South-East Asia, and after its cessation many innovations began to make themselves felt in the prosperous Straits Settlements and the Federated Malay States. Roads were built to accommodate the motorcars and lorries linking hitherto isolated communities. Aircraft opened up new possibilities for travelling, while the arrival of sound broadcasting meant that news travelled in minutes instead of weeks and months. In short, communications were the touchpoint which made these areas more comfortable and prosperous places for the well-to-do of all races, than they had ever been before. The Japanese invasion was to shatter it all forever, for the shock of the collapse was to cause not just a loss of face for the armed forces of the so-called impregnable Singapore, but a loss of faith in the ability of the right arm of the British, which was never again to regain its former power. In the biography of Lee Kuan Yew, the present

Prime Minister of Singapore, Alex Joncey records that it was the spectacle of this fall from power, which gave a Japanese soldier the facility to strike Lee in the face with a rifle butt and to push his friends into a lorry to be driven to their execution, that made Lee resolve that never again would his country be dependent upon a foreign power. However one looks at it, the Second World War was a salutary lesson to many of us, and its effects will be felt for a thousand years to come. . . .

When peace returned in 1945, the British suggested a new plan for a National State called the Malayan Union. It proposed the unification of all the nine Malay States with Malacca and Penang with all that that involved, and it proposed a common citizenship, in itself seemingly a good idea. But it would have destroyed the special position, negotiated so long ago on tradition and treaty, of the Malays, and also removed the autonomy of each Ruler, reducing them all to religious leaders. The Malays, already jealous of the Chinese and Indians for their undoubted mastery in business affairs, rose as a man in protest, and it was then that the first Malayan Nationalist Party came into being. Errors in the new proposals were speedily acknowledged and changed, and in February 1948 the Federation of Malaya came into being with a clear pledge of self-government and a free system of elections as soon as possible. (Singapore's self-government was a separate issue.)

But a new and far greater danger was on its way. In 1948, the Malayan Communist Party went 'underground' into the jungle, with the avowed intent of setting up a communist republic. They began immediately with their programme of terror, killing, maiming, burning, destroying all and anything which even faintly stood in opposition. As in every war, the brunt fell on small, poor, helpless people going about their lawful work in the rubber and pineapple plantations and isolated farmlands, and they were terrorised into giving the communists assistance by examples of awful reprisal. But it must be said here that there were also a lot of sympathisers forming a kind of fifth column. To protect the innocent, and immobilise the not-so-innocent, over a half a million country people, most of them Chinese, were resettled in five hundred new villages, guarded day and night, and in order to maintain the policy of denying food to the communists, over forty thousand people were fed from central kitchens. This is not the place to discuss the rights and wrongs of the campaign, nor to dwell on the dangers and difficulties of life under the Emergency. It is enough for me to say that travelling in Malaya at that time and living on the perimeter, as I did, was an object-lesson which will stay in my memory as long as life lasts.

In 1952, when Sir Gerald Templar, was appointed as High Commissioner, the Emergency was at its height. His directive from London stated that 'The British Government will not lay aside their responsibilities in Malaya until they are satisfied that Communist terrorism has been defeated.' By 1955, the firm policies of British and Commonwealth forces in the jungle war were winning and London relayed its feelings to Kuala Lumpur suggesting that self-government was now in sight. The difficulties of Malaysian citizenship had mostly been ironed out earlier, and when the 1955 elections had taken place in July of that year, there was an overwhelming victory for the Triple Alliance, which meant a multi-racial government with Tunku Abdul Rahman, leader of the Alliance and president of UMNO, as Chief Minister. He led the Mission to London for the talks and on 8th February 1956, he signed the Merdeka Agreement with Lennox-Boyd, the then Secretary of State for the Colonies. It was a moment of triumph for this Prince of the ruling house of Kedah, but it must also have been tinged with regret on one issue. A bare six weeks earlier, on 28th December 1955, he had met Chin Peng, Secretary General of the Malayan Communist Party at Baling, a few miles from the Malayan/Siamese border, together with Mr. David Marshall, the then Chief Minister of Singapore, and Dato Sir Cheng Lock Tan, president of the Malayan Chinese Association. The Tunku had hoped that with the knowledge that Independence, or Merdeka (Freedom) as it was termed, was being given, Chin Peng would cease operations against the hated 'British oppressors', on promise of an amnesty for the terrorists. But Chin Peng demanded recognition for the Communist Party. The Tunku categorically refused this and Chin Peng returned to the jungle on the Siamese border, where he still is to this day. After he signed the Merdeka Agreement, the Tunku ordered the anti-communist measures to be intensified, and the amnesty withdrawn. In recent years the terrorists have again become something of a menace in the northern States, but Malaysia is just as firm as the British once were, and intends to root them out wherever they re-appear.

Singapore's steps towards self-government had been proceeding at the same time as those of Malaysia. By March 1951 there had been two general elections and the communists had tried to infiltrate into Singaporean life without much success, because the island afforded little shelter for gunmen, and only in the slums could they find the right breeding grounds for their doctrines. In addition the fractionalisation of the Chinese communities into so many Secret Societies, still in the manner of their forefathers – a system which has existed for a thousand years and more and is likely to continue for a long long time yet – didn't leave that much room for Marxist or Leninist ideas, though of course, they gained some ground among the malcontents. The People's Action Party, led by Lee Kuan Yew, was formed in 1954 and in the 1955 elections won three of the four seats they had contested. By 1959, they had won 43 of the 51 seats, and after the release of certain political detainees, Lee Kuan Yew became Prime Minister of Singapore, a post which, at the time of writing (1976), he still holds. In December 1959 Inche Yusof bin Ishak, the first Malayan Head of State, was installed in office, and the present Singapore was fully operational.

Many people, certainly the majority of the white population of Singapore and a considerable number of well-to-do Chinese and Indians, at that time looked upon Lee Kuan Yew as communist, but events proved that this was not the case, although he has walked seemingly hand-in-hand with them on various occasions. Instead, he has led his predominantly Chinese population into a highly successful socialist State, and improved the lot of many of the poorer people. However, in the ungrateful way of humanity everywhere, some of the sweeping reforms haven't always met with universal approval, particularly when the reluctant recipients 'didn't want to be done good to'. . . . In 1963, he also led them into a marriage with Malaysia, but the honeymoon only lasted two years and was dissolved by mutual consent. The other 'wives', Sabah and Sarawak, married at the same time to Malaysia, have remained within the family. The divorce was probably an inevitability, with so many widely differing viewpoints and longstanding jealousies, but one must regret the severing of ties between cousins. As long as the rift is not allowed to widen with petty irritations and the constant temptations to score one against another, little harm will be done, but the situation is, I am certain, under constant review by both sides.

The differences are indeed longstanding, and are based in the racial characteristics which are highlighted when peoples reach nationhood on their own account. One must not labour under the delusion that the Chinese and Indian communities, both of which have large stakes in Malaysia as well as in Singapore, are 'johnny come latelies'. As we have seen, both races were in the area from the beginnings of recorded time. But in view of the necessity to understand the position a little better even for a brief holiday or business visit to Malaysia and/or Singapore, let us look further into the background. In Singapore's case, it was not until after Raffles founded his city that overseas Chinese started to arrive in large numbers, setting up in business as merchants of all kinds. This was obviously of interest to Raffles, for when he started to replan Singapore he was already aware not only of difficulties between the mixtures of races making their home in the island, but also between sections within the Chinese communities. These were caused, as in every part of the world in every nation, by the different tongues, dialects and customs, and even in the early days, by the Secret Societies, which had inevitably come from China with them. He therefore divided the city into areas, and this can still be seen today in street names which have been retained. Chinese continued to arrive in great numbers, fleeing from a land overburdened with petty officialdom and tortured by famine and war. In the years between 1895 and 1927, millions of Chinese came, bringing cultures, ingenuity, business acumen and their own languages. In 1906, they set up the Chinese Chamber of Commerce to cope with particular problems engendered by their internal differences, and they have stayed unmistakably and irrevocably 'Chinese'. Today, in the tiny shop houses tucked under the shoulders of the skyscrapers which threaten to overwhelm even the sluggish waters of Singapore River, you can find the remnants of the unmistakable atmosphere of Old China, and see what early Singapore must have been like.

The problems in Malaysia are and were slightly different. It is not known exactly when tin-ore deposits were first worked, for there have always been Chinese miners and traders, but Arab writers referred to its presence as early as the ninth century, and Chinese records during the early part of the 15th century said that there was tin beyond Malacca and that men were being sent to mine it. In Perak, most of the mining was done by Malays, but in the early part of the nineteenth century there were already about 400 Chinese miners there. When a Malay discovered tin in Larut and obtained permission from the Sultan to mine, there were only three Chinese reported in the area, but large-scale migration, mostly from mainland China, soon followed. By 1862, the numbers were between 20,000 and 25,000, and by 1872, there were nearer 40,000. The majority were Cantonese, but there were also a number of Hakkas. The two sections fought like fury over the ownership of mines and piracy was rife. Eventually the British had to partition the land, as Raffles had partitioned his city. Although right from the beginning it was Chinese capitalists who worked with imported and indentured labour, it was not only in mines that the Chinese community swelled and prospered. They were originally charcoal burners, then brickmakers and contractors, traders, shopkeepers and shippers, and thousands of them became coolies, opening up the rich lands hidden in the hinterlands. Naturally they multiplied, and now, Chinese represent roughly 42 per cent of the entire population of Malaysia. Although many parents and grandparents were Chinaborn, the majority of today's Chinese were born in Malaysia. Their thinking and allegiances are to that country and there are fewer and fewer contacts with mainland China. A similar situation applies among the two million or so Chinese in Singapore for the great majority of these were 'Straits-born' as indeed their Prime Minister is. The Peninsular Straits-born Chinese are still known as Nonyas and Babas, and one can recognise them by their adoption, in so many instances, of Malay dress. One can understand that with the addition of Singapore in the formative years of the new Malaysia, the Malay communities were concerned that they would be swamped by the thriving, industrious and extremely fertile Chinese section of the population. Some of this fear has now been eradicated, but there are still occasional signs of it. It is bound to take time. Let us hope that it doesn't take more time than is available for complete unity.

People are particularly conscious of the fact that they must get over this mistrust of each other. They know that they must try to make a unity lost by their elders, possibly through no fault of their own, but by circumstances which have arisen during this last 40 years. But still people do remain in their different communities and though in the new blocks of flats different races live side by side, there are still very distinct settlements for each racial group. When talking to younger people, they express the opinion that there should be far more mixing of peoples and are hopeful that it *will* take place because most of their generations wish it to happen. There are still Indian settlements too, and although these minorities do not represent the same problem, it is necessary to look at their appearance on the scene, for they play a very important role in economic development. When Sir Henry Wickham smuggled seeds from the Brazilian rubber trees to the royal Botanic Gardens at Kew in the 1870s, no one would have associated this highly unorthodox procedure with a change in the racial structures of far off Malaya. In 1877, 22 of the saplings from the Brazilian seeds were sent East, to be shared between the

Botanic Gardens in Singapore, the Residency Gardens in Kuala Kangsar, and Trong in Perak. They flowered and matured, but the latex couldn't be extracted without killing the trees. The man who solved the problem was Henry Nicholas Ridley, the Director of the Botanic Gardens for Straits Settlements at the end of the 19th century. Despite his recommendations that his precious trees could be farmed to provide an extremely valuable crop and his habit of carrying seed around in his pockets begging the scornful planters to try them (which earned him the epithet of Rubber Ridley), he had no takers. Then Nature took a hand. The coffee plantations which until then had carried one of the main crops in the Peninsula, were attacked by blight. It was, I understand, the Beehawk Moth. At almost the same moment, the motor-car industry was finding its feet in the western world and planters, desperately seeking a way to fend off financial disaster, decided to try the erstwhile despised rubber. Now, as we have already seen, there had been Indian communities living in Malaya for centuries and their Hindu religion had been the universal one until the advent of Mohammedanism, but they had mainly confined their activities to trading at ports along the coastal strip. The planters, most of whom had come to Malaya from Ceylon, preferred to use Indian labour, as they had done in their Ceylonese estates, so they imported Tamils and Sinhalese to work the latex in the herringbone methods devised by Ridley. This immediately increased the Indian population in Malaya by a considerable degree. The men were indentured for several years, living in housing on the estates and sending their money home to support the relations left behind. Despite the presence of the Coastal communities of Indians, the life was a lonely one for the newcomers deep in the interior, and gradually, families joined them, retaining the customs they had known in faraway India, and making little islands of Hindu cultures within Malaya's green heart. There was also a considerable amount of intermarriage. After all the Malays and Indians had a common religious, and to an extent a common historic background. Today, the Indians comprise about ten per cent of the population of Malaysia. There are many wealthy men among them in commercial enterprises of every kind from moneylending to tailoring, as well as many workers still in the rubber plantations where it all began, but even today the ties with Mother India are very strong and money is sent home to families as it has always been.

In Singapore, when the first census was held in January 1824, five years after the founding, there were 756 Indians living in the new city. Most of them were convict labour – 'Klings' as they were called in despatches and reports – although there were also 'Bengalees'. Much later, they were joined by clerks, shopkeepers and others and, as they had been educated in the English manner in India a small number of them eventually found their way into local government administration. It was natural that, in a colony where many of the white civil and military officers had had long associations in the Indian sub-continent, Indians, many Sikhs among them, were recruited into the police forces as well as into British Army units. At the present time (1976), there are about 150,000 Indians in Singapore representing approximately 7% of the population. The most interesting point is that, whereas the other racial communities have a fairly even balance between the sexes, the Indians still have a preponderance of men. It might take a number of years to change the patterns started at the beginning of the present century.

These three races, therefore, Malay, Chinese and Indian are the ones which have come to be regarded as the main communities in Malaysia and Singapore, but there are many minorities: Europeans, Arabs, Pakistanis, Jews and Armenians, as well as endless permutations of all of them, products of the mixed marriages which are an inevitability when so many races live in proximity for a long time. I find all and every one of them fascinating and am entirely in agreement with the comments of Isabella Bird, when she wrote 'The women are, I think, beautiful, not so much in face as in form and carriage. I am never weary of watching and admiring their inimitable grace of movement. Their faces are oval, their foreheads low, their eyes dark and liquid ... It is only the European part of Singapore which is dull' . . . and then . . . 'what thinks she, I wonder, of the pale European?'. . . .

I could perhaps, answer her with a true story.

Many years ago, when we lived in Singapore, my golden-haired three-year-old daughter was playing with her bosom friends, Carol, a blonde like herself, and Halima, a little coffee-coloured beauty who was the granddaughter of a much loved and respected Malay amah. Some time later, we were horrified to see all three emerging from a disused garage, the two Europeans, much bespattered with red enamel, and carrying a paintbrush, and Halima, bright red from head to foot. After the inevitable and protracted cleansing programmes had been carried out, and retribution inflicted on all three alike, we, mothers and grandmother, asked 'why'. The answer was simple, and hardly flattering to the 'white' race.

'Halima was fed up with being brown, and wanted to be bright red, like us.'

2. Wheels, Water and Wings

'The port of Singapore is a free port and the trade thereof is open to ships and vessels of every nation, free of duty, equally and alike to all.' When Sir Thomas Stamford Raffles made that pronouncement he was referring to the traffic which, in his day, came almost exclusively by sea, but I like to think that if he returned to Singapore today, he would be extremely pleased at the position that it holds in the transport systems in South-East Asia. It would confirm again, if confirmation was necessary, that his choice of the island for its accessibility and future potential was a wise one. Over two million people visit Singapore each year and approximately 100,000 of these are tourists. Nearly a million and a quarter travellers find their way to Malaysia and a large percentage of these are holiday visitors also. This is a far cry indeed from the arrival of Admiral Cheng Ho in Malacca in 1405, or that of the two Englishmen and a sepoy at the mouth of Singapore River in 1819, but I believe that many of today's visitors are not just in search of sun, sea, cheap shopping and a change of horizon, although there is a multiplicity of these, but are also bent on discovering more about some of the most fascinating lands in the Far East, in the limited time at their disposal. One glance around the National Museums in Singapore and Kuala Lumpur confirms that people like to look backward as well as forward. To see as much as possible in one short holiday frequently entails the use of varying forms of transport in order to fit into tight schedules, and so often one just catches a ship or a plane, or a railway train without knowing anything at all about how it happened to be available at the moment one needed it. The abundance of such facilities in today's world has been the life's work of many of our fellow creatures and it may be that part of a voyage of discovery could be enhanced by even a minimal amount of pre-knowledge. Without the great companies, British and Chinese, whose financial interests in every kind of trading, including, latterly, rubber and tin, depended on the availability of safe, free harbours and good communications between East and West, neither Malaysia nor Singapore would have reached their present world status. The oceans were the first, and for a long time, the only way in which the world could find Malaysia's shores and one cannot talk of transport in this area without referring to this background of shipping. Nowadays vast numbers of people use jet travel and this enables a bird's-eye look, in more ways than one, at many places previously not reached by coastal routes. For instance, one way into Malaysia and Singapore which is widely used is via Bangkok which enables one to combine the trip with a stopover in this, one of the most intriguing cities in South-East Asia, and it is quite a logical progression, for so much of Malaya's early history as we have seen was intermingled with that of Siam. Indeed, it was necessary for me to take a Thai International flight to Bangkok to start my own excursion into the pages of time with which this book had of necessity to start, to visit the museums there before going on to Kuala Lumpur. It occurred to me then that this was an exciting new dimension which, if it had been possible to use earlier, might well have resulted in not having anything to write about at all! So perhaps we should be thankful that man has taken his time with much of his discovery. . . .

It was a tremendous contrast to my first introduction to South-East Asia, which, like so many expatriates before me, had been from the deck of a ship in the great P. & O. fleet, sailing the time-honoured route via Suez, Aden, India, Ceylon, Penang and the Malacca Straits before coming to roost in Singapore for a day or two before the onward voyage to Japan. That was a gentler introduction to a way of life which had heretofore been an unknown to me and it allowed a slower metamorphosis, something which the jet world, with all its marvels, could never do. Long ocean voyages have become a thing of the past except for the luckier, wealthier and more leisured among us who can take time to join world cruises and know the excitement of new ports as they slip gently in and out of our ken, and one tends to forget – but in 1975 when I arrived once more in Singapore through her water gate at the end of a marvellous trip around Indonesia, I experienced anew the magic moment of arrival in her exotic, bustling Roads, and I remembered ... *Canton, Chusan, Himalaya* ... and all their whiteclad sisters whose advent was always marked in red letters in the calendars of Colonial Singapore.

The Peninsular Steam Navigation Company was established in Britain in 1837, and was not, as many people imagine, named for the Malay Peninsula, but for the peninsula of Spain and Portugal. Support for the Royal causes in civil wars gave the company the right to fly the royal standards of those countries, and the house flag to this day is composed of the red and yellow of Spain and the blue and white of Portugal. (The 'Oriental' was added in 1840 when the company had won an Admiralty contract to ply between Gibraltar and Alexandria.) In 1845, the P. & O. contracted for the China mail, via Ceylon, Singapore and Hong Kong, and the first mail steamer to arrive in Singapore was the *Lady Mary Wood*. The date was 4 August, and the letters had taken 41 days to reach their destination. Not bad when one considers that the central part of the journey was still overland, for, from Alexandria, passengers had to disembark and cross the desert by coach to the Gulf of Suez. There they re-embarked in another vessel bound for India. By 1848, we find passengers writing to the newspapers to complain of the service, and blaming the shortcomings on the 'monopoly', saying that there was an exclusive concern for their own interests and a complete disregard for those of others. A year later in the *Madras Times*, someone commented, 'I am of the opinion that it is derogatory to the dignity of human nature to submit to be treated like a bale of cotton.' Obviously he would never have survived the London

Underground in the rush hour, Incidentally, a 'gentleman's' fare was about £95 for a shared cabin between Southampton and Singapore. It was 'slightly more' for a lady. No comment. . . .

The 700 ton *Chusan* was the first steam- ship to complete the Australia/Singapore run, and a ball was held in the Agents new house on New Harbour. The ship was dressed overall in fairylights and there was a firework display on board. Knowing Singapore's predilection for firecrackers until they were banned by the present Government, *Chusan* was lucky to escape mishap. With the opening of the Suez Canal in 1869, the long Cape Route became a thing of the past, but in connection with Suez it is noteworthy that when Arthur Anderson, a prime mover in the founding of P. & O., travelled the overland route in 1841, he reported to the Foreign Secretary on his return that a ship canal was a perfectly feasible undertaking. But that was contrary to popular belief at the time and no notice was taken. The French were more enterprising and constructed the Canal, so that it was eventually a French ship, *Aigle*, with Empress Eugenie on board which made the first voyage through it.

The changed routes meant that ships came down the Straits of Malacca from Penang and the traffic in Singapore doubled in five years. There was a certain amount of acid comment in Straits papers on the failure of P. & O. to take full advantage of the Canal, comparison to French mail service, in which the luckless British came off much worse, and loud demands for new ships to accommodate the constant flow of expatriates to and from the Colony, a flow which included Civil Servants, Military Personnel and planters as well as individuals joining the rapidly expanding merchant houses, or who were setting up in business for themselves in the booming city. While reading some of these letters to the papers, I reflected that people don't change much, for during my sojourn in Singapore there were constant and lively discussions on the relative merits of ships and lines for they were still part and parcel of the way of life. But, with the coming of Merdeka in Malaysia and later in Singapore and the gradual Malayanisation of jobs, there was no further requirements for the transport of large numbers of personnel back and forth to the U. K. and in any case the jet age tolled the death knell for the long haul passenger liners. They were taken off the run, some to be sold, some scrapped and some, like *Himalaya* and *Canberra* adapted for service as one class cruise liners. It is still possible to make the three week journey by sea if one has the time and money, but far more people fly out to Singapore as I did to join *Prinsendam* to join cruise liners which spend all their days in the warmer climes.

There are also regular ocean services between Singapore and Australia which can be reached by regular flights from Europe, and sometimes, all too seldom for lovers of nostalgia, one sees the familiar quartered flag of Peninsular and Orient arriving on a positioning voyage and remembers that it is part and parcel of the very fabric of South East Asia.

The practice of taking a ship around the coasts is still a very popular one, whether on a brief harbour cruise, a visit to offshore islands, or on longer voyages up and down the Straits of Malacca. After all, a deck is one of the coolest places in the humidity of the tropics, as well as one of the most romantic when the moon hangs so large and so low above the phosphorescent waters that one can almost touch it. . . . It must have been a most attractive proposition long before the advent of air-conditioning, when, in 1843, the steamship *Victoria* made her experimental cruise from Singapore to Penang, Malacca and return. Cabin passengers were charged one hundred Straits Dollars for the round trip, provisions included, and the announcement in the Singapore Free Press stated 'If it is found that the expenditure so incurred is not so great as at present anticipated, a modification of the rates will be made in future.' Looking at these costs, today's fares of approximately six times that amount for a five day cruise on *Rasa Sayang* is not excessive, particularly when one takes into account the ever present pirate menace in the middle of the nineteenth century. This activity has always been the province of Malays and Bugis, and it didn't cease with the advent of the British, or indeed with Independence, though nowadays piracy takes

rather a different form! It isn't without some piquancy that
one learns that the Temenggong who signed the Treaty with
Raffles had, until that date, been in the habit of getting a
rake-off on booty, prize monies, female captives, etc., and I
cannot honestly conceive that he would have changed the
habits of a lifetime just because a few Britons arrived. It didn't
help the situation either when Chinese pirates joined the
jackal pack in 1853, and there was also the occasional ques-
tion of mutiny and murder on the High Seas. In 1848 Jardine
Mathieson's *General Wood* was on her way from Hong Kong to
Bombay with cargo, passengers and Chinese convicts. She'd
left Singapore for Penang, when somehow the convicts were
freed; they murdered the captain, many passengers and
seamen, and attempted to sail back to China, but without
much success. It was hardly the best way to see the Straits of
Malacca, particularly for one English lady, a Mrs. Seymour.
She wasn't harmed, but her husband suffered some attentions
from the pirates. He was thrown overboard and only saved
himself by hanging grimly to a dangling rope's end for hours.

It took the combined efforts of British and Dutch to rid the
area of pirates (or so it is claimed) by the 1880s. Smuggling
however, was rather different, and is still widely practised.
The shallow-built, high-speed launches of the Customs Departments, fitted with sophisticated tracking equipment
know their way around and over every piece of coral in the
archipelago while chasing the men who make a living from
trafficking in illegal cargoes, but despite the vigilance, and the
extremely heavy fines and sentences particularly when drugs
are involved, a certain amount still gets through.

Links with the more recent past are constant and inevitable. Among the first European names in the formation of
Singapore was a certain W. R. Paterson. He formed a company in 1842, then went into partnership with a Mr. McEwan
which gave birth to the Borneo Company. Royal Charter was
received in 1856, and one of the first directors between that
year and 1874 was a John Templar, an ancestor of Sir Gerald
Templar who was to figure so importantly in Emergency years
in Malaya. Many of the Borneo Company's early records were

lost during the London Blitz in the Second World War, but to-day, the Company is as powerful as ever within the Inchcape Group, and, due to a recent merger, owns 45 per cent of the cruise liner *Rasa Sayang*, the aforementioned cruising liner from Singapore! I think this proves my point that a visitor, if he wishes, can find a feeling of continuity, however tenuous. . . .

For the sealoving tourist with a few days to spare, there is another wonderful way of travelling, This is by the vessels of the Straits Steamship Company who have a number of first class passenger berths on their diverse routes up and down the Coast and to Sabah, Sarawak and Brunei. These voyages give an opportunity to see the ports in a different dimension, much as traders have done for generations, and the ships themselves stem from the marrow on which the great Straits traditions were built. Although the present Straits Steamship Company was formed in 1890, its roots go far deeper. It was around 1770 that a Fukien, Tan Hay Kwan, came to Malacca to join the rapidly expanding Chinese community. He brought his junk, and, when the British came to Penang, he traded there and founded a family business. His grandsons introduced steam to the family ships and it was their nephew, Tan Keong Saik, who eventually brought three vessels into the founding of the present company. Another Tan from Malacca had come South to Singapore when it was founded in 1819 and had set up an import/export business in his forenames, Kim Seng. Not unnaturally, he became shipping Agent for the other Tans, and in due course his grandson, Tan Jiak Kim, took over. He too joined with Theodore Bogaardt of Mansfields in founding the Straits Steamship Co., and in so doing brought about a natural merging of some of the most powerful Chinese and British shipping interests in South-East Asia. Like every other company in the area, they lost a lot of shipping in the Second World War, and today's fleet is therefore of a reasonably modern generation. Their routes each have their own enchantment but there is a similarity in the scenic attractions, although when approaching Kuching, capital of Sabah, through the pattern of islands all of it is played out against a far off background of Kota Kinabalu. There are palmfringed beaches where the stilted fishermen's villages perch above the water like ruffled storks, and small brown children tumble, or stand, gazing with slumbrous eyes at the passing ship ... fishing *kelongs* paddle in the deeper waters festooned with the nets of their calling and beyond the coral, wallowing junks, small *prahus*, grubby tramps, all of them dressed overall with their crew's laundry ... and as the wake charts a frothy white curve across the murky amber and jade water, great globs of jellyfish undulate and disappear. A Dutch engineer told me once that the Java Sea is one of the most polluted in the world and I can well believe it for it has been traversed since humanity disovered how to float on the waters, and man is notoriously a dirty animal. Because of this, it is even more pleasing to see just how much progress has been made in Singapore's attempts to clean up her Roads in what is still the fourth largest port in the world. The aroma isn't quite as pungent as it used to be, but even so one can still distinguish when the tide is out, and come dúrian season when the husks lie discarded in the turgid water between the sampans it is still highly desirable not to have too sensitive a nose.... But ... durian or not, at this moment, as I write in the chill of an English winter, I would give a great deal to be sitting on the deck of a Sarawak-bound steamer as she leaves Singapore on the tide. ... From some of the ports up and down the Peninsula there are opportunities for short trips on the tiny craft that go out to the many islands; Singapore is particularly well placed in this respect.

In a Far Eastern daybreak, life itself seems to hold its breath, as if the whole world suspends activity for one brief moment, and allows mankind to savour its beauty. For those who, like me, dislike sleeping in airconditioned rooms and prefer the thicker atmosphere of natural tropical air, the moment of dawning is pleasurably cool, and one shivers slightly in the faint breeze which stirs the verandah 'chicks' so that they slap gently against the pillars. The sound drifts through the silent house ... time to get up, for days start early in the East and the traffic can already be heard on the roads at the end of the drive. The crickets chirrup in endless unsyncopation in the Lallang grass and in the distance, bullfrogs croak their final salute before the mynah birds waken to take over the day shift. I slip into my car, still mercifully free from the fierce heat which transforms it into a mobile sweatbox later in the day, and drive out to Paya Lebar to catch Singapore Airlines' plane to Kuala Lumpur, and even as I do, a brassy sun surmounts the horizon, warming one's arms through the open window as if to warn that, within half an hour, the pristine cotton dress will be concealing a band of perspiration around one's middle and there is even moisture in one's shoes. By the time we take off, the sun is high and the erstwhile spurned air-conditioning is more than welcome. Little cotton-wool clouds flick by beside us, hiding the highrise buildings, remnants of virgin forest and the red laterite of the cleared land. The sea and causeway are below, so too are the harbour installations along Johore Strait, while road ribbons flutter inexorably northwards towards a hot, hot day. . . .

Flying never loses its thrill for me however much I travel, but I think if I live to be a hundred I shall never forget the very first time I took a morning flight to Kuala Lumpur in 1957, or my first glimpse of the Malayan jungle humping under a dark green eiderdown like a Victorian maiden reluctant even to reveal one glimpse of the naked flesh of its rounded buttocks. I thought then that this was one of the most beautiful lands that I had ever seen, and time and worldwandering hasn't changed my opinion. Climate has, of course, a great deal to do with Malaysia's modesty. Grass grows so fast that it must be cut daily, and even building scars are soon decently concealed by a mantle of new green, so that despite a considerable amount of construction work the land remains clothed from a distance. For the traveller by today's planes, flying higher and faster, the panorama remains unspoiled, and flying is an ideal way to see much more of the country than is otherwise possible in a brief holiday or business visit, and both Malaysian Airline System and Singapore Airlines provide invaluable service in this respect.

It is only since 1972 that Singapore Airlines has become an

operational entity in its own right, but its experience is by no means that of a small, young airline, for before that time many of her employees wore the insignia of the combined airline of Malaysia and Singapore, so that once more the two nations have a mutual history. Air travel has come a long way since the time when Spirit of Australia, piloted by Captain Hurley, landed in Seletar in 1928. Singapore was visited by Amy Johnson too when she landed there in her Gypsy Moth in 1930 and, according to the *Straits Times*, 'was welcomed sedately by a small crowd of about two hundred'. On 16th April 1931, the Imperial Airways DH66 *City of Cairo* arrived with the first British Air Mail from U.K. and, says the same indefatigable and unimpeachable source, 'three to four hundred people all tense with excitement', waited for her. Indeed the reporter waxed quite poetic. 'She circled the aerodrome once and having got her bearings, sank gracefully to earth outlined against a typical Malayan sunset, some two hundred yards from the fringe of the waiting crowd.' She took off next day for Batavia, piloted by Captains Mollard and Alger, but it was an adventurous business in those days, and buffeted by strong headwinds and short of petrol, they crash-landed at Koepang. Luckily there was no injury to anybody, and the Dutch Post Office took charge of the precious mail until Kingsford Smith and his co-pilot, Allan, arrived in the famous *Southern Cross* to take it on to its final destination in Australia. However, these hadn't been the first airborne excursions into South-East Asia by a long chalk, for K.L.M. the Royal Dutch Airline, had pioneered their flights into Batavia (now Jakarta) from Amsterdam as long previously as October 1924, and in May 1933, when they brought a connecting service into Singapore with a Fokker Aircraft, it was a good seven months earlier than the Imperial Airways inaugural flight on 9th. December so that KLM can rightly claim to have played an extremely vital role in the development of air transportation into Malaysia and Singapore.

It was the newly-named Qantas Empire Airways, formed in 1934, who operated the Singapore/Brisbane section of the England/Australia route, with Imperial Airways retaining the

London/Singapore run. By 1938, three Qantas/Imperial Airways Short Empire flying boats called each week into the Singapore base. It was already obvious to some longsighted people that aircraft were to be an important ingredient in transport arrangements for Far Eastern routes and that Singapore might well prove to be essential to air traffic as it had been to traditional sea routes. Therefore it should have just as good servicing in its airport facilities. And it wouldn't only mean traffic for Singapore. The Malay Peninsula could be covered with feeder services, and there could be new routes into Sarawak and Borneo as well. In 1936, two Australians, C. and T. Wearne, who ran a bus service within Malaya, bought two De Haviland planes and formed Wearne's Air Services with a thrice weekly service between Singapore and Penang via Kuala Lumpur. They commenced the service in June 1937 and within three months increased the flights to a daily basis. By 1939 they were looking into the possibilities of flights into Kuching, despite certain trials and tribulations with various Government departments. The war stopped all progress, as it stopped so much else, and the company ceased operating in December 1941. But you will still see the name Wearne very much in evidence in ground transport in Malaysia.

Other names too crop up again and again in the pedigrees of both Malaysia and Singapore. The Straits Steamship Co. Ltd., the Ocean Steamship Co. Ltd. of Liverpool (Blue Funnel Line) and Imperial Airways, came together in 1937 to form Malayan Airways, but the company wasn't airborne before the Japanese invasion came, and it was ten years later, on 2nd April 1947, that the first passenger-paying flight was made by five Chinese businessmen. It was followed some weeks later by the first scheduled flight between Singapore and Kuala Lumpur. The planes in use were little Airspeed Consuls, and they covered a network which linked Singapore, Kuala Lumpur, Ipoh and Penang by a daily flight, with Kuantan and Kota Bahru included once a week. The advent of the Emergency in 1948 brought Malayan Airways into its own. Road travel was a hazardous business, and in any case air travel was no more expensive than the railway at that time.

Later on, as I remember very well, they even took on the job of dropping pay packets to isolated rubber plantations, so that one can say that air transport had arrived well and truly in Malaysia. Incidentally, during those twelve years, a rather interesting personality became the General Manager. This was Captain Roger Mollard, that same Mollard who had piloted the *City of Cairo* to Seletar in 1931. I always believed that Roger had a personal acquaintance with the top of every rubber tree on the Peninsula and in Borneo, and that having someone with such tremendous personal experience behind him must have helped enormously with the successful operation of Malayan Airways.

When Singapore's new airport at Paya Lebar was opened on 20th August 1955 it was one of the largest in South-East Asia. Until then Kallang had been used, an airport which had been built on drained swampland, and now transformed into a pleasant recreational and residential area with a superb stadium. Paya Lebar has been extended considerably with impressive terminal buildings, but it has been outgrown in its turn by the sheer volume of traffic which flows through it, and by the unwisdom of allowing it to be surrounded by industrial developments which have prevented its expansion. With the withdrawal of British troops from Singapore, Changi has been rather idle for a long time, and now has been designated to be the site of the new Singapore airport. The first phase should be completed by 1980. But my affections, I think, will always be for Paya Lebar, and for the many people who have been working there ever since its inception. On my last visit, I walked into an office to enquire for someone, but before I could give my name, a voice behind me gave it for me . . . and I turned to recognise an Indian handyman who had made my daughter's dollshouse in his spare time, sixteen years before. I'm not sure who was more pleased at the reunion, particularly when I told him that the dollshouse was still as good as new, and put away for future owners to take charge. . . .

In 1958, as Independence from Britain came closer, there was an important milestone for Malayan Airways. Qantas supplied on lease a Douglas DC4 which enabled the commencement of a Singapore/Hong Kong route, the first time that the young airline had climbed up into the international league. It was on that Douglas that I visited Hong Kong for the first time. It was an excellent little service, but even then we were forced to skirt around the trouble spots of Vietnam, looking so deceptively peaceful in the distance, until we came finally to the tricky descent on the flight path that pilots had to follow between the mountains into Kai Tak. By pure coincidence, I made a similar journey from Singapore last year by the first Singapore Airlines Jumbo on the route. It took half the time, at twice the height, the flight was as smooth as silk, and we whispered effortlessly down that flight path to land on the extended runway at Kai Tak. But the service on board was the same: impeccable, courteous, but with time for every passenger. Despite my overwhelming nostalgia for yesterday, I was very, very happy to know that the manners of the mother airline had rubbed off on one of her daughters.

When international expansions continued in 1959 most of the money came from BOAC and Qantas, although the Governments of Malaysia and Brunei had stakes, but by 1966 the respective Governments of Malaysia/Singapore, as it was then known had much bigger interests. The airline prospered, but there were very big differences at high level within the company. These were but a reflection of the coolness which had developed between the two nations, but in addition there were arguments about the future objectives. Singapore, with her dependence on overseas trading lifelines, considered that international advancement was vital. Malaysia wanted, not unnaturally, to further domestic networks so that her economic development could grow both in the Peninsula and in the islands. It provided a good excuse to part company without loss of face on either side . . . a state of affairs which is sometimes overlooked by personnel unfamiliar with the habits of people in this region, but which is of paramount importance. Malaysian Airline System and Singapore Airlines became operational in October 1972, and since that time have developed in healthy competition. MAS has improved and extended its domestic routing so that many otherwise isolated towns can be included in the itinerary of any visitor to Malaysia with a minimum difficulty, and the entire length of the country can be covered in a day if required, although for me, that smacks far too much of 'If it's Tuesday it's Malaysia' and is not to be encouraged! Inevitably MAS has not confined its activities to Malaysia and has considerable international routing, while Singapore Airlines has also gone from strength to strength. Although still dependent on the business traffic which brings the bread and butter into the Island City, Singapore Airlines has wisely concentrated a lot of attention on tourist potential and the immense possibilities on her doorstep. At the time of writing (1976), SIA is not yet a Member of IATA, but is likely to be accepted in the near future. Perhaps that will have happened by the time this book is printed. It might also be the final sign that Singapore has, at long last, grown out of her longstanding image as the Mecca of the entrepreneur and of the entrepot trades, as the Door to High Adventure and the Lair of the Pirate, and has assumed the mantle of complete respectability. I still find it sad to contemplate, however inevitable.

Railway travel in Malaysia is easy and comfortable, for the system reaches over the whole Peninsula, across to Singapore and up to Bangkok, with the appropriate national changes of course. One can go to Bangkok from Kuala Lumpur in two days for approximately 100 Malay Dollars for a First Class ticket (1977). If you plan to do this journey, be sure to have a visa with which to cross the land border, and take it with you when you leave the United Kingdom. Otherwise a lot of time can be wasted hanging about in offices in Kuala Lumpur or Singapore. Between these two latter places you can use a comfortable overnight train, the Southern Cross. This has always been a popular service because it has a good restaurant car and bar aboard, and indeed is a most civilised way to travel. But if you want a daylight journey, the Rapid Express takes just under six hours on its daily run. The North Star to Penang can also be taken if required, but advance reservation of sleeping berths is almost mandatory. Many years ago this was *the* main land route between the Straits Colonies. While researching for this book, I came across a splendid manual issued in 1928 by the Federated Malay States Railways (the name given to the unified railways in 1910 and which lasted until the Japanese invasion), giving the through first class fare for the 24 hour journey between Penang to Singapore as 31 Malay Dollars, which was then the equivalent of £3.12.6. . . . £3.62½pence. Yet it isn't all that long ago . . . not yet 50 years.

The Railway systems in Malaysia have evolved over a long period and naturally stemmed from economic necessity. Athough the first railway in Malaya was eight miles of track running between Taiping and Port Weld in 1884, the first paying line was that constructed between Kuala Lumpur and Klang, and as soon as it was opened it earned a profit of 25% on its capital. In spite of this shining example, it wasn't until 1903 that the main line ran through all the Western States from Seramban in Negri Sembilan to the terminus opposite Penang Island, at Prai. Later the Negri Sembilan section extended to Johore, via Malacca, with a terminus at Johore Bahru, exactly opposite that of the Singapore railway over the Strait of Johore. But Singapore was no quicker in its adoption of the iron horse. From 1872 onwards the most remarkable arguments and manipulations raged in the Colony, and it wasn't until the turn of the century that a line was built which ran to Kranji. It was 1923, when the Causeway was built, that the rail link to the Peninsula was finally completed. This link facilitated the exportation of Malayan rubber and tin through the Singapore Docks, and this continued right until Malaysia's own ports were extended and improved at Port Swettenham, now renamed Pelabohan Klang. Naturally, the railways weren't built and didn't run through virgin jungle without some adventures. Once, an elephant charged a railway engine at Telok Anson with catastrophic results to himself. There used to be a signboard at that spot on the line, which records the place where he is buried and it read that in defence of his herd he charged and derailed a train on 17th September 1894. I don't know if it is still there. But his skull is in the museum in Kuala Lumpur, and beside it there is an interesting little story which reads as follows:

'It is historically true that on a single line, a train rounded a curve and hit an elephant, The train was derailed and the elephant's body was flung by the train into a storm drain alongside the railway embankment. But no one with any knowledge of wild Malayan elephants believes that the elephant charged in defence of the herd, for bulls rarely travel with the cows and play no part in their defence. They run at the first sign of danger and gladly leave the protection of the herd to courageous old females like Grandmothers and Aunties. The bull on the Telok Anson line was certainly no exception, yet, for decades he has been regarded as an elephant hero. He was the only elephant in the world with his own obituary notice, so a doubtful chapter of railway history was made by a lone bull who wandered on to the line and failed to get off in time, or, as seems more likely, by an imaginative engine driver who didn't keep a good lookout and had to find a plausible and romantic explanation which would appeal to his superiors of why he ran his train into an elephant.' (An extract from a book called *The Company of Animals*, by Ronald McKie.)

As far as I am concerned, I like the elephant story. It seems a shame to take the credit away from the old chap now, so I'll keep on thinking of him as a Brave little Bull. . . .

The East Coast lines were also opened up in the first half of the present century and now one can catch the romantically named Golden Blowpipe which runs three times a week between Gemas and Tumpat via Kuala Lipis. It is probably the most spectacular ride by rail in Malaysia, for it enables one to see the 'triple canopy forest' otherwise hardly visible to the ordinary traveller. In Sabah, there is another interesting possibility for the railway buff. If you assemble four or more companions to yourself, you can charter a railcar to run on the Sabah State Railways between Kota Kinabalu and Tenom, which gives some tremendous views of jungle and the tumbling mass of magnificent water of the Padus rapids.

Every visitor to Malaysia and Singapore remarks sooner or later upon the excellent road systems which make it very easy indeed for motorists to wander at will. There is no doubt that it is the finest way to see this wonderful country leisurely and at close quarters and, even around the main cities, a car can make a lot of difference to one's sightseeing programmes. Singapore is excellently served with good road surfaces, but traffic is heavy. Kuala Lumpur has some splendid freeways on its approaches, particularly from the airport, but even its ordinary roads are wellsurfaced, and have correctly placed monsoon drains. This is, incidentally a hazard that the unwary and inexperienced tropical driver should take into consideration. Many a newcomer has ended up with a broken axle through forgetting the presence of a drain when parking, but one soon gets used to leaving the necessary room. There are plenty of car hire firms plying both in Singapore and in Kuala Lumpur and elsewhere for spontaneous hire, and in addition there are some fly/drive schemes available from Britain which are an excellent package buy for the footloose brigade who prefer to find their own accommodation en route. This is not difficult to do, providing one doesn't expect five star hotels at *every* stop. The best bets for a trip of this kind are, in my opinion, the Rest Houses. They provide simple accommodation and good food at reasonable cost, but naturally local people are well aware of this facility and the rest houses are often full with pre-bookings. It might be an idea to plan an itinerary if you are thinking of this sort of journey through Malaysia and write out to try to make some arrangements at least at a few of your intended stopping places. But, if you are prepared to take pot luck, then you should try to make for the bigger towns, as I have indicated in my chapter on the East Coast.

I think that no one in Malaysia would dipute that they owe their road systems to the British influence. Until the advent of roads, the mail was still carried by steamers, for to do otherwise entailed the use of runners through jungle and, where possible, pony carts along the tracks laid down from the tin mines deep into the jungle and far from the coasts. British residents saw that the road construction was a priority if the States were to expand and develop into the modern age. Funds were very small, though money was borrowed from the Crown Colony of Singapore for the purpose. The difficulties of ploughing up hill and down dale were immense. Sir Frank

Swettenham, that invaluable and inimitable purveyor of information on Malaya tells us that six foot bridle roads were introduced into Selangor in 1882/3. They had no metalling, but had good gradients and simple bridges and cost about £150 per mile. As soon as practicable the earth road was converted into a metalled type and the bridges made permanent. He claims with some justification that if the latter type had been put in in the first instance it would have cost ten times as much. Naturally enough as soon as a road of any sort appeared, villages (kampongs) sprang up beside it and inevitably the land increased in value. As there were few men rich enough to find their own finance, and mine and agricultural settlement was essential, the Government gave loans to immigrants to help business to get started. Sir Frank is on record as saying that 'all advances made to Chinese were faithfully repaid'. . . . In the fullness of time, villages gave way to towns, with schools, hospitals, markets and all the other appurtenances of community living, and so we see the present setup whereby almost all of the towns, hamlets and kampongs lie within easy reach of the road systems available. Inevitably expansion inwards will take place and new roads laid down, in Malaysia at least, though I feel that Singapore has more than its share now. The road between Penang and the East Coast should have been in use by now, but due to various delays and setbacks, not least the terrorist activities still indulged in by Chin Peng and his merry men, this project has had to be postponed for the time being. But it will be completed, Malaysia is determined on that, and to that end is still pursuing the policy of crushing the nuisance wherever it arises. Let us hope they can do it soon. That road would make all the difference to tourists bent on seeing 'all Malaysia' from the seat of a car and, most important, it would put the hitherto isolated East Coast in direct connection with the Penang and West Coast ports. I can't help thinking that the very first traders who crossed the Isthmus so long ago, would smile wryly to think that this is still the final road to be built. . . . Apart from this road, there is no violent hurry for the others, except possibly for a swifter road between the capital, and the East Coast and this is being undertaken along the present routes at the moment. Even around its biggest towns, Malaysia has a lot of room to build without necessarily damaging the character of the countryside. Perhaps this spaciousness will in time prove to be her greatest asset.

For those without cars but still desiring to go by road rather than rail, sea or air, there are regular coaches connecting Singapore, Kuala Lumpur and other cities and towns. Some of them are on public transport systems, others are privately owned. The Mara coaches are good, and airconditioned. All are reasonably fast, and fairly cheap, but I would stress that journeys by coach are not for the easily wearied, for they can be long and tiring, particularly through the heat of the day. One sits in a puddle of perspiration almost from starting out, without airconditioning, and cools down almost too much with it. One needs stamina for Malaysian buses, and even more of it for the Land Rovers which serve the same purpose in Sabah and Sarawak.

One other way of journeying long distances is in taxis. One usually puts these in the gold plated class, but in Malaysia everybody uses them. One goes to the taxi stations and a driver calls out his destination. When he has four passengers, the taxi goes nonstop and the passengers share the fare between them. You can actually travel all the way from the Thai border to Singapore by this method, though I must admit I still haven't plucked up courage to use the system for more than a few miles. However, one of these days. . . .

Taxis within towns are reasonably speedy and are metered, though if you want to go out, from, say Orchard Road Hotels in Singapore, to Pasir Panjang where Tiger Balm Gardens are or out to Jurong, it is better to negotiate a rate with the driver for him to wait for you. Remember that on normal runs the meter starts ticking from the time the taxi leaves the rank if summoned to a hotel. Many drivers speak good English, and if you talk to them, you'll learn a lot about the places you pass, or about the people themselves. What will perhaps surprise you, if you happen to see it, is the method of cleaning out taxis. It can be drastic in some cases, for one often sees a hose stuck inside the vehicle to wash the upholstery. It dries quickly in the hot sun, but it does account for the musty smell one often gets. However, it is a lot better than the smell of cockroaches so often encountered in other parts of the East.

Buses within towns are also quite efficient, but don't expect them to be luxurious. Most are rather ramshackle, but they have the great advantage of being the cheapest way of getting from A to B. In Singapore, you will find a bus to almost anywhere from Empress Square, and indeed in the rush hour or in rain, when taxis are like gold dust, it can be quicker to catch a bus to the hotel districts than to wait despite the queues.

Finally, no one could leave the subject of transport without mentioning that most ubiquitous of vehicles, the tri-shaw. This is a bicycle with a sidecar, powered entirely by the sturdy legs of the cyclist. It took the place of the rickshaw in Malaysia and Singapore, though one still sees these occasionally in Hong Kong and universally in Macau. Tri-shaws were my small daughter's favourite form of transport in Singapore and she knew most of our local ones by name. This was due to her propensity for trotting off, with a small friend in tow, to visit the food hawkers in Happy Valley – usually just before lunch when we'd taken our eyes off her for five minutes. The Chinese love children, so they were safe enough, and the kids were always brought home by beaming tri-shaw drivers, usually eating some particularly gooey forms of Chinese sweets donated by their hawker friends. Needless to say they were all tipped very well, but it became very amusing, not to say embarrassing when we went out in style on occasion in an official car with our daughter in her very best dress. She waved like Royalty from the back seat, and a progression of gold-teethed, coolie-hatted brown faces smiled back, calling 'Hallo Missy'.

. . . I can't guarantee you the same treatment but you must try the system. Fix your price *before* boarding. You, after all are a tourist, and haven't got a Mum to pay up at the other end. . . !

3. Starting Point, Kuala Lumpur

'It always rains when I come to Kuala Lumpur'. That thought darted through my head as I crossed the tarmacadam from the Thai aircraft which had brought me from Bangkok to Malaysia. But there, the resemblance to any previous visit to the airport which serves Malaysia's capital ended, for Subang is one of the most pleasing and impressive air terminals in South-East Asia with handsome airport buildings and great expanses of gleaming floors and glass partitions, and with sheltered curving inclines for passengers' use, to reach custom halls and luggage collection points. It is far different from the rather informal little field which graced Kuala Lumpur not long ago, and is quite a starting point to present day Malaysia.

Another starting point for some visitors to K. L., as it is always popularly termed, is to arrive at Port Klang by ship, travelling inland from there. Better known to many British as Port Swettenham, Pernamboh Klang as been given an expensive facelift to bring its harbour facilities to a level suited to its position as the Capital's port. It was not only vanity that engendered the expenditure of such large sums. It was also due to the blow hot, blow cold relationship with Singapore, which spurred Malaysia to obtain another gateway other than her neighbour's docks, for with Penang, and Klang, Malaysia could be completely independent.

Port Klang, too, must look far different to the place from which the group of miner-explorers who first braved the crocodile infested waters of Klang River set out to reach the rich earth housing the precious tin of Selangor State. They arrived at a muddy estuary, where the Klang joined forces with the Gombak. Indeed that is the direct translation of Kuala Lumpur . . . muddy estuary.

Crocodiles weren't the only hazard. Malaria claimed even more victims and of the 87 Chinese miners who had come with the expedition, led by R Raja Jumaat, Raja Abdullah and two Chinese businessmen from Malacca, only 18 survived to continue overland to the point where Ampang is today. That is, just beyond the racecourse, and it was there that they found the rich deposits for which they searched. As we have already remarked, most of the tin miners were Chinese. Life in China had been so difficult that hard living conditions didn't worry them unduly. They were tough, rough men, addicted to gambling and opium, and divided into gangs in whose wars murder and theft were commonplace.

They were a law unto themselves, and Sir Frank Swettenham tells of a conversation with one gang captain who pointed to a table and said 'that is where I pay for the heads of the enemy. Every head brought in and placed on that table is worth one hundred dollars and sometimes it has been as much as I could do to count the money fast enough'. It became the practice for the Sultan to appoint the most powerful of these Chinese captains to keep the peace, and gave him the title of Kapitan China. Yap Ah Loy was the third of these. He had arrived in Malacca in 1854 at the age of seventeen, and he rose to be the most powerful Chinese in Selangor. He built a prison, flung the worst offenders in it, and succeeded in bringing a semblance of peace and a rough justice to the new township that it had not known before. There is a street named after him in today's city, and in Jalan Rodger, there is a temple to which he donated money and lands. If you are curious to see what he looked like, go to an altar at the rear of the temple, for there is a picture of him there.

By 1884, plans had been put in hand to build a railway between K.L. and the port of Klang, and it was opened in 1886 with an inaugural journey by the Sultan. After this time the town began to have its present form. Prosperity brought businessmen and merchants and they built splendid houses along Ampang Road, and by 1895, Kuala Lumpur was named the capital of the Federation, which at that time consisted of Selangor, Negri Sembilan, Perak and Pahang. Even so, K.L. remained a quiet country city in spite of its impressive new Secretariat buildings completed in 1897. This was two and a half years after the cornerstone was laid and is quite a remarkable achievement when one remembers that architects and craftsmen were all imported. The Railway Station was built at about the same time, and it is these buildings which have stamped their impression in K.L. for the rest of time, for they look Moorish, as, in a way, befits the capital of a Moslem country.

Today, Kuala Lumpur changes daily as motorways, flyovers, highrise hotels and shopping complexes force the nation headlong towards the 21st century, but its great redeeming feature is that it has remained an open city, with large areas of parks and gardens within its boundaries, a precious commodity for any capital. Credit for this must to a large extent be given to the earlier planners. For instance, the Lake Gardens, now quite a feature of K.L. in tourist literature, cover an area of about 160 acres to the south of the centre of the city, and were commenced by a Mr. A. H. Venning on behalf of the Government of the day in 1888. In ten years the work had been completed and the gardens were officialy opened by the Governor. Sydney Lake, or Tasik Perdana as it is now called, the centrepiece, is artificial, though one would never dream it to be so, but growth is lush in Malaysia and the rate at which plants reach maturity is a gardener's dream, or a nightmare if one has to keep it all in order. Grass, even coarse lallang, must be cut daily and weeds removed immediately or the primeval jungle creeps back within weeks. The Gardens have therefore reached a maturity which makes them look as if they have been there 'for ever', and it is beside this lovely setting that several modern and important buildings have been placed. We will deal with these a little later in the chapter.

On my most recent visit to Kuala Lumpur, I was lucky enough to arrive on the eve of the Prophet Muhammad's birthday, celebrated with some ceremony and rated as a public holiday . . . a commodity of which Malaysia has a very ample supply, for each community has many special days of its own. This is a most convenient arrangement for the rest of the population, for then everybody else takes the day off too. Christmas, for instance, celebrated by the Christians in the community is given a terrific importance by the other religions. The best Christmas cards usually come from the Moslems or Chinese among one's friends along with enormous Christmas presents. Conversely when it is Chinese New Year, the rest of the population give 'ang pows' the traditional gift wrapped in red paper – to all their Chinese friends, so the whole holiday situation in Malaysia and Singapore is a highly satifactory affair all round. There are so many holidays in the South-East Asian calendar that your visit is bound to coincide with one or more of them, so go . . . and find out for yourself.

I was up betimes to attend the rally in the Merdeka Stadium, held in the presence of the Yang di-Pertuan Agong, the King of Malaysia, who is, at the moment H. M. Tuanku Yahya Petra, Sultan of Kelantan. (The rulers have an amicable arrangement whereby they all take a turn at being king for five years.) I had been in the stadium once before. That had been during the ceremonies to mark Malaysia's Independence, and it had been one of the most emotionally disturbing moments that I can remember. This time Saudi, my mentor, and I parked the car a little way from the stadium and joined the hundreds of people, dressed in their best, who walked up through the gardens in the cool of the morning. Big events usually take place around seven a.m. before the heat of the day takes over, but already the sun was high. Many of the men were wearing the white songkok which indicates that they have made the pilgrimage to Mecca and are entitled to be called 'Haji' in respect. Most were Malays, but there was a goodly sprinkling of Indians too. The main area of the stadium was rapidly filling with small groups holding brilliantly coloured banners proclaiming their club, or organisation, such as Scouts, Guides, Workers Clubs, nurses, and so forth. The bands played, and the people sang, and occasionally shouted slogans when encouraged so to do by a cheer leader. It was all very reminiscent of a Cup Final . . . then the religious significance took over and prayers were intoned and suddenly it became more like Remembrance Day. It was an impressive sight on that golden morning and it became even more so when, sheltered by the yellow silk umbrellas of Royalty, the King descended from the Dais into the arena and walked at the head of the procession from the stadium through the streets towards the mosque. It was the right atmosphere in which to start a new journey through Malaysia, and, as I watched from my vantage point, snippets from the past flicked unbidden into my mind.

I was at the presentation of degrees at the University of Malaya in Merdeka Year of 1957, and as always I had been more fascinated by the people around me than by the pomp and ceremony on the platform. These were families, Chinese, Indian, Eurasian, Malays, of the boys and girls who had worked so hard towards this, their graduation day, and I'll never forget one man. He was an old, old Malay, dressed for the occasion in his ceremonial sarong and songkok, made of the glittering and expensive kain songket reserved for the most important occasions in a Malay's life. He sat, motionless, impassive, until one name was read out. Then as I watched surreptitiously, I saw a slight change in the old man. He sat straighter, prouder and there was something akin to a tear in his eye, though I am equally certain he would never have admitted it. I wondered now, while standing in the stadium, just where that son or, more likely, that grandson had fitted into this new nation. Perhaps, somewhere in this crowd in 1976, he was there, somewhere. . . .

One of the very nice things about Malaysia is the fact that there is complete religious freedom. Everyone may worship in his own way, or not, as he wishes. The national religion, however, is Islam and one of the most spectacular buildings in South-East Asia is Malaysia's National Mosque, Masjid Negara. It took five years and ten million Malay Dollars to construct it, and it was opened in 1965. It looks across to the Railway Station, and it is strange, really, for the Railway Station has the architecture that one usually associates with a

Mosque, while the Mosque resembles nothing so much as a vision of outer space. Foreign visitors are allowed, but women non-believers are expected to don one of the long black robes, something like a schoolmaster's gown, which hang in readiness along racks at the entrance stairs, and, of course, one must remove footwear before entering the holy ground. The shaded verandahs are wonderfully cool as one passes the gurgling fountains and the shining marble terraces caress one's feet. The Grand Hall is the heart of the building. This room has a high umbrella shaped dome, pleated like a seashell, and is decorated with an eighteen-pointed star. This represents the 13 States of Malaysia and the five pillars of Islam. The whole is supported on 16 beautifully proportioned columns. The floor is close carpeted for the faithful to kneel and I am told that it can accommodate, together with the verandahs, somewhere in the region of 8000 people. We walked along one of the verandahs to the far end to the mausoleum where the great men of Malaysia have their place, much as the heroes of Britain go to Westminster Abbey or St. Paul's. My visit was shortly after the sad death of Tunku Abdul Razak, Prime Minister of Malaysia, in the London Clinic. His body had been brought back to Malaysia and interred at the Mausoleum, and his grave was covered in flowers. Tunku Abdul Razak played a considerable part in Malaysia's peaceful path towards self-determination and in her progress after it, and he richly deserved the honour his countrymen have accorded to him after his death.

As I left the mosque, it was the hour for muezzin. Saudi was about to start the car, but I stopped him. We sat, wrapped each in our own thoughts as the lonely voice echoed and re-echoed from the tall minaret, over the silent mosque and the tranquil gardens and into the city, and, when it eventually died into silence for the last time, we still sat for moments before making ready to start again in the hurly burly of everyday existence.

Religious beliefs, birthday celebrations or national holidays apart, the best place to get an exceptionally good idea of all Malaysia has been, is, or is likely to be, is in the National

Museum. This is one of the buildings now situated in the area of the Lake Gardens and was built, at a cost of a million and a half Malay dollars. It was opened in August 1963 and is impressive with its sloping roofs and enormous murals. These show episodes in Malaysia's history as well as a selection of arts and crafts. The murals were donated to the Museum by the late Dato Lee Kong Chian, a former Chancellor of the University of Singapore. They cost the Dato something in the region of 135,000 Malay Dollars, a not inconsiderable sum for one man to give, even though a millionaire. I had the privilege of knowing him. A charming, courteous and extremely considerate gentleman, who always had a battery of pencils, like a schoolboy, in the pocket of his frequently untidy suit, he must be placed among the great Chinese of his generation, not because he made money, or even because he was generous with it for things he believed in, but because he never allowed it to dominate his own personality.

Inside the Museum is a wealth of detail of every aspect of Malaysia's past. For example, for generations, there was far more importance attached to a circumcision ceremony for a Malay's sons than to his wedding and the panoply surrounding it was far more elaborate and colourful. This is still so in some places. The last Royal occasion on which this ceremony was observed was in Kelantan in 1932, and all the paraphernalia attached to it can be seen in the Museum. The young prince was carried in procession on a mythical bird called a Petali Wati, and he arrived in front of the circumcision pavilion, given the name Balai Sunat, which was part of the Royal Palace. His arrival had to be greeted by five persons, the Court Circumciser, the Umbrella Bearer, a lady in waiting, and two elderly palace officials. The Umbrella Bearer conducted the Prince to the pavilion, and the lady in waiting scattered yellow rice over him and the ceremonial bed. The Court Circumciser had to carry out the operation with speed and efficiency under the watchful eyes of the two trusted officials who were armed with long swords, and, if he injured the prince, he was liable to be executed there and then. Hardly conducive to a steady hand. The panel in the pavilion in the

Museum was designed from traditional motifs, and the big 'burong' (bird) associated with circumcision, stands beside it. All the bird's feathers are made of silver, gold and blue paper and the wings of palm leaves. On its back is the traditional howdah in which the small prince would have been carried to his ordeal. And inevitably, the yellow umbrella, symbol of royalty since Cheng Ho brought it from his Emperor in China, is in evidence near the models.

There is a great deal in this museum, models show top spinning, Bersilat (self-defence, Malay style) and the martial arts, and other aspects of Malay culture. One interesting display is of musical instruments. In the States of Kedah, Perak, Trengganu and Selangor, there are groups of traditional instuments which are maintained by the rulers, and these may only be played by royal command by certain members of the retinue. Usually these are hereditary duties. In these States, the ruler is installed to the sound of the Nobat, as it is called. This ancient custom, which dates back to fifteenth century Malacca, has been adopted by the Yang di-Pertuan Agong, and in fact, the Kedah Nobat played at the wedding ceremonies of the then king's daughter in 1962. Much of the dancing traditions of Malaysia seem to have overtones of Cambodia, so obviously they must have made their way down the entire length of the Peninsula.

Another interesting exhibit is the table used at the signing of the Pangkor Treaty, and it was brought to the K. L. National Museum from the Taiping museum, where it rested for a long time. It was made specifically for the meeting between the rulers and conferences were held around it for four days, between 16th and 20th January 1874, on board *Pluto*, a steamship anchored off Pangkor Island. Part of the reason for the Treaty was the desire to put an end to the Secret Society wars in Larut. They had got so bad that 1000 Chinese had been killed in a single day, but when the Treaty was eventually signed on 20th January 1874, it was the beginning of direct British intervention in the Malay States, and the end of the open feuding between the tongs.

There are some particularly fascinating details about the

Trengganu stone. This was found in 1902 half buried in a river bank, 20 miles inland from Kuala Trengganu, when there had been a flood which had washed away the silt of centuries. The inscription is Arabic, but is in the Malay language. Some letters are dated as 1303, which makes it the oldest Malay inscription in Arabic in existence which has so far been discovered in Peninsular Malaysia. It is also the oldest contemporary record of Islam, for the inscription promulgates Islam as the official religion and records the Moslem law in regard to false evidence, wantonness, etc, and also sets out the scale of punishment for people of different rank. Part of this stone was missing when it was discovered. Who knows whether another flood will uncover the rest?

Try and find time to visit the Natural History section of the museum if you can. It shows all the species of bird, animal, insect, fish, etc which used to, or still do, live in Malaysia. It is well worth spending an hour of two there if you intend to be in Malaysia's National Parks for any length of time, for the visit will help in speedier identification of creatures you may encounter. And, of course, you will find the Telok Anson elephant's skull mentioned earlier, proving that he has earned his place in the nation's progress.

Not far from the National Museum, and still in the Lake Gardens area, is Malaysia's National Monument. One doesn't see many tourists here, apart from the occasional Briton. But then, we have a special pride in the men of Malaysia who fought beside us so gallantly and faithfully, and wish to honour them along with our own dead. The Malays have honoured us in turn, in the memorial plaques along the shaded porticos. The central bronze memorial is a beautiful piece of work, standing 20 feet high, and depicts men of the armed forces. It is surrounded by a pool, with a cascading fountain circles by water lilies cast in pewter. Not long ago the statue was terribly mutilated by someone who didn't like what it stood for, or its form, and it was undergoing repair at the time of my last visit. Perhaps the vandal would have been better employed in remembering that without the sacrifice that his countrymen made, he would never have had the freedom to protest at anything. When the Memorial Gardens were completed, the Cenotaph, which for long had stood near the centre of K.L. and which remembers the dead of two World Wars, was brought up to the Lake Gardens It looks towards the 18 storey Parliament House which is also now installed in this area of K. L. I have a feeling that the men whose names appear on the sides of the Cenotaph might not be displeased with their transfer to this beautiful and tranquil setting.

For visitors with limited time to spare, but desirous of seeing something of Malaysia's important resources, Kuala Lumpur can be a useful stopping point. From its hotels, it is but a short drive to the tin mines, and rubber estates, both of which have been the main reasons, along with palm oil, for the country's prosperity. Rubber estates are somewhat disappointing when only seen from the road. They are such tidy places, with trees planted in neat rows disappearing into infinity in the shadowed interior of the estates. You will notice that most of the trees bear a series of cuts on their bark, and dependent on the time of day, you may see the cup which catches the latex, suspended below the most recent cut. The tappers, Tamils and Chinese mostly, work on the trees in the very early morning, so by mid morning the estates have a deserted air, but later, usually before noon, you can also see workers emptying the latex cups and transporting the liquid latex in yoked buckets to the factory for processing. It is transformed into rough sheets and placed in the sun to dry, before departing to the mills. If you are anxious to see the process in detail, I would suggest that you contact one of the tour operators who can arrange this for you. Mayflower Acme have comprehensive coverage of the subject. It requires some time, but it is well worth while, if for no other reason than to walk in the lonely plantations where shadows leap, to realise how easy it was for the trees to be slashed and destroyed during the Emergency, and to feel what it must have been like to be one of those plantation workers who were at the mercy of the terrorists and were injured, tortured and murdered in an attempt to force them into helping the communists. It is only when faced with actuality that one can even begin to understand the tremendous problems which faced authority during those years, and which are, indeed, never far from the minds of the present government should the pressures increase again.

You could leave looking at the tin mines until a day when you can combine them with a visit to the Batu Caves, which, in my opinion are a must if you are in the vicinity of Kuala Lumpur. An American can claim the distinction of discovering them, for it was a naturalist, William Hornaby, accompanied by a Briton, the Selangor Chief of Police Mr. H. E. Syers, who, when out riding one hot afternoon in 1878, came to the foot of a large cliff. The air was putrid, enough to turn you and I in the other direction, but Hornaby recognised the smell as bat guano and knew that somewhere near, there must be a cave, and that, in turn, could mean fresh specimens of insects. He dismounted and started to climb the almost vertical cliff face, until he reached the group of caves some 40 feet above the ground. Sure enough, there were new species there, and in the years since that momentous day, no less than 50 hitherto unsuspected creatures have been discovered. One of these was a spider which had long been believed to be extinct, and another was a cricket, which, believe it or not, is 'lord of the ants'. It seems to have some power of communication with them for scientists have found that the ants react to certain gestures made by the cricket by bringing food. Another inhabitant is an assassin bug, which kills its prey with a bite from a mouth like a bayonet. Yet another is a scorpion which has every attribute of its species apart from the sting, (as a Scorpio I was rather relieved to find that there is one of us with less unkind ways! . . .) and many more. But every one of these creatures depends upon the existence of the countless bats which roost in the caves and have no less than nine different species among their own numbers. But there is far more to the several caves than natural phenomena. Shortly after the caves were discovered, local Hindus set up a shrine to their deities within the Main Cave and the one to Lord Murugan has been the centrepiece of the annual Thaipusam festival ever since.

This is one of the most remarkable sights to be afforded to the visitor, and although it can be witnessed at the main Hindu Temples in Singapore and in Malaysia, if you can see the ceremony and procession at the Batu Caves, it will be something to be remembered all your life. Let's look a little closer at the meaning of the festival before proceeding any further with an exploration of the caves, for it will help with what you see there.

The name Thaipusam means tenth month in the Hindu calendar, and the passing of the full moon across Pusam. According to Hindu mythology, once upon a time the world was ruled by twin evil forces. But, one day, the Lord Murugan was given a spear by his mother Parvati, which was to overthrow them. That day was Thaipusam. Ever since, it has been an occasion for the fulfilment of vows made, and penitence to be undergone, and the way in which this is done is to carry a kavadis. This is a very heavy structure, usually of metal, decorated with bright ribbons and flowers. It is carried on the body by means of sharp needles and spears which pierce the skin quite deeply. In addition, extra penance is undertaken by the use of long sharp skewers which are passed through both cheeks and through the tongue, and I have seen small cups being carried on sharp hooks in the flesh of back and chest. Prior to the day of procession, the penitent has to attend instruction from the temple priests to prepare him for the ordeal. By the time he arrives at the starting point, he seems to be in some state of trance and is always surrounded by a dancing, chanting crowd of friends and relatives, encouraging and urging him onward. The journey ends for him in front of the statue of Lord Subramanium, when the kavadis is removed and ash is daubed on the wounds. The strange thing is that no bleeding occurs and afterwards there is no scar of any kind. One of the members of the family of an Indian friend of mine in Singapore vowed that he would carry a kavadis if his little daughter was made well of a seemingly fatal illness. When she recovered, he did go in procession as promised, and there was no sign afterwards of his ordeal. I had many discussions with Indian friends, among them medicos, in Singapore when I worked at Sata Clinic. They could offer no explanation except that the state of shock brought about by the trance stopped the feeling of pain and the flow of blood temporarily. But, for the lack of scars from what must have been quite large holes in the flesh, they had no explanation. At least, none that they could or would give to me.

At first, the caves were reached by a flight of wooden steps, but the stone ones were built in 1940. There are 250 of them to the Dark Cave, and then a further 42. On my first visit to the Batu Caves, I walked up every one of them, as the penitents do, and in Malaysia's humid heat, that is quite a feat even without the kavadis headgear. Since 1974 however, one can do it the easy way, for a cable car has been installed, which helps the impenitent among us quite considerably. The ticket for the car includes admission to the Caves. If you walk you still have to pay at the top. The Main Cave is the one directly ahead of the top of the cable car up the 45 steps, and this is the cave used by Hindus as a shrine. At the far end, the cave opens to daylight and one is in a kind of natural bowl of ragged cliff. It is a grubby, dank place with little to recommend it, but it is a mandatory part of the tour, and, should you be there at a period after the Thaipusam festival, you will see piles of discarded kavadis frames still lying where their weary owners have flung them. On my last visit, I was fortunate enough to arrive at the shrine at the same time as a newly wed couple who came to be blessed. It was quite amusing really, for they caught the priest unawares, with his feet up and reading a newspaper. I was reminded of making a call on our vicar once and finding him in similar circumstances.

The Dark Cave is very different. It used to be a very difficult place in which to walk and only a really zealous and skilled veteran in cave exploration would have ventured within its depths . . . or foolhardy journalists in search of copy. . . . In 1955 a skeleton was found within the cave; a signed message on the wall said that the writer came from China and, in 1940, had entered the cave to commit suicide through starvation. His last request was that the person finding his remains would add his name also. The Japanese used the cave during the

Second World War and the Allies found it an impossible task to winkle them out. Nowadays, exploration is simple, for in 1973 a covered two-way footpath was installed which can be followed for most of the 1200 feet of the length of the cave. Why covered? Otherwise one is the constant and unwilling recipient of guano from the bat populations living four hundred feet above, and it smells enough on the surrounding rocks, let alone on one's clothes. What it must have smelt like when the guano was processed, by roasting, into fertiliser, I dare not think.

In the information pamphlet for Travellers published in 1928 by the Federated Malay Railways, there is some reference to the caves. It said that one could 'take the train to the Caves,' for the line was built to serve the limestone quarry near to them as well as to the railway workshops en route. One 'followed a path through the rubber plantation where if it be early you will pass coolies tapping the trees. This leads to the steps for the caves and a somewhat steep pull lands you under the outer arch.' After describing the caves it says about returning: 'halfway down the steps is a rough track to the right which leads to another cave inhabited by bats, white snakes, frogs, toads and a very vile smell. It is dark and dirty walking and should only be attempted with a guide and lights.' Changed days indeed as we stand on the platform at the top of the cable car track and see the constant procession of visitors, including a horde of schoolchildren making their way to the showcases of specimens and to the Gallery Cave now devoted to details of the Hindu religion. The Caves are at once beautiful and repellent, but the latter comes almost entirely from their association with Man. Finally, while at the top of the steps, look, as the 1928 pamphlet recommended, at the view. You will see gashes made by the tin mines, and on the way back to K. L. you could stop for a closer look at the huge dredger. After all, tin was the *raison d'être* for K. L.'s existence. The tin is mined in many ways, gravel pump, open cast, dredge and dulang washing, but in all of them water is the principal mining agent, for it is used to wash the tin ore free. One word of warning. Don't go too near to the actual mining ground, for the soil is mostly loose sand and can be dangerous.

Generally speaking it will depend on your own itinerary when travelling in Malaysia on what you should buy in K. L. If you have no time to go to the home of the various industries, such as Batik, Silver and Brass, found on the East Coast, or to Penang, or down to Singapore where most things are very much cheaper than K. L., then you can buy well in almost any store in the city. There are so many of them now, mostly in tall new shopping complexes. Very convenient, but one loses the individual atmosphere and it is hardly possible to tell which country one is in by the designs either. However, don't buy anything until you've had a look at all the shops in your vicinity. Prices vary a great deal, often according to the whim of the shopkeeper that morning. In Jalan Tuanku Abdul Rahman however, you'll find the Mara Building, and all the Malaysian arts and crafts can be found there, in addition to imports from Indonesia, Thailand and elsewhere. Further along the same road is the showroom of the Selangor Pewter company but if you are really set on taking some of their products home with you, and very beautiful they are, go to their Demonstration Showroom at 101, Jalan Gentin Klang, Setapak, just outside the city. All the taxi drivers know it, and will wait for you. Apart from the lovely things on show, such as tankards, vases, plates etc, there is a display showing the various stages of production, from the tin ingots to the final hammering or polishing of the finished item, and one can learn all sorts of things about the history of this fascinating and versatile metal. During the 18th and 19th centuries, it was usual for tinminers, whether Malay or Chinese, to ensure an auspicious start for a new mine by means of animal sacrifices to propitiate the local demons. So that the necessary magical ceremonies might be undertaken correctly, the miners employed a magician called a Pawang, to supervise the smelting of the ore. There was a widely held belief that tin was possessed by a 'sole' spirit, and was therefore subject to control by ceremonial incantational magic, and, the first tin dug from a new mine was cast into a pair of shellbacked ingots to which magical properties were attributed. In time, each ingot acquired a head and four legs which gave it the appearance of a tortoise, a creature whose shellmarkings were believed to represent a message from the spirit world. Eventually other animals and insects such as elephant, crocodile, fighting cock and grasshoppers were added, which were adopted as substitutes for the living animals. In Pahang for example, they formed part of the traditional presents to royalty, and their general desirability led to their acceptance on a limited scale as internal currency, though in Kedah, only ingots in the shape of fighting cocks were accepted as currency. There are examples of these ingots on show in the Demonstration rooms. Other exhibits include pictures and models of the tinworks, dredging palongs etc, and they have also a large pair of boxing gloves made in pewter. These were made to commemorate the World Heavyweight Title Fight between Muhammad Ali and Joe Bugner in K. L. on 1st July 1975. The showroom is usually packed with tourists, but prices are reasonable and if you are after pewter souvenirs either to take with you or send home, this is the best place to go.

Wisma Loke, the former home of Towkey Loke Yew (Towkey is an expression meaning big boss!) was the first private home in Kuala Lumpur to be lit by electricity and was built by a contemporary of Yap Ah Loy, called Cheow Ay Yeok. It has Chinese porcelain balustrades and Malacca tiling. It is now a showroom for antiques, as well as an artists' gallery. But although the shops and showrooms are very good, and comfortable places in which to shop at leisure, the best fun is in buying from the stall holders who are legion in K. L. and your bargains will depend a lot on your own quick wits. The Sunday market takes place (on Saturday night!) in Kampong Bahru, and this is the best place of all for food, knick-knacks, souvenirs etc. In fact everything except the very expensive items which should only be bought in reputable stores. You can eat in Kampong Bahru too, if you don't want to use a smart restaurant. There is also an array of good eating stalls in Jalan Campbell between the cinema and the police station, and in Jalan Brickfields, beyond the YMCA

1. *East Coast market scene: prawn seller*

2. *Batik painting, East Coast*

3. *Sarawak: the Satok Bridge which carries pedestrians and water pipes over the river at Kuching*

4. *The 272 steps to the Batu Caves, Kuala Lumpur*

5. *Kuala Lumpur's municipal buildings*

6. *The Stadthuys, Malacca, dates from the days of Dutch influence*
7. *East Coast: coconut baboon*

8. (*top left*) *Penang: the Pagoda of* 1000 *Buddhas, Kek Lok Si Temple*
9. (*bottom left*) *Birth of a new generation at Snake Temple, Penang*
10. *The main streets in Panang still look a little old-world*
11. *Penang Hill Railway climbs to 2722 foot summit*

12. (*top left*) *Interior of longhouse, Ensebang*
13. (*bottom left*) *Children are always in evidence in longhouses*
14. *Headman dancing on longhouse, Sarawak*
15. *Fine feathers make fine birds: dancers at Ensebang longhouse*

16. (*top left*) *Market place in Sabah*

17. (*bottom left*) *Ferry boats and fishing boats in Kuching, Sarawak.*

18. *Mount Kinabalu's 13,455 feet towers above the clouds: view from Menkabong, Sabah*

19. *Street scene in Singapore*
20. *(top right) Squid on market food stall, Singapore*
21. *(bottom right) The old and the new from Singapore River*

22. *Laughing Buddha in the Tiger Balm Gardens, Singapore*
23. *Chinese medium in a trance in a Singapore temple*

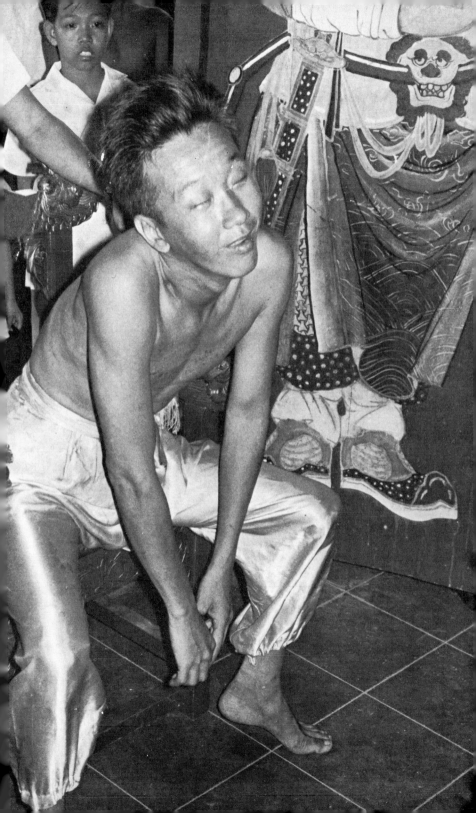

24. *Rubber tapper at work*

and the Railway Station, but to taste satay at its best, there is only one place to go. This is to Kajang, 14 miles from Kuala Lumpur on the Malacca road. Satay is small pieces of chicken, beef or lamb, barbecued on sticks and served with peanut chili sauce. I don't know why Kajang satay is best, but I think it must be the sauce. You order the type of satay you require and leave everything to the waiter. He'll bring a huge array to the table, but you don't pay for it all. Eat what you want, then, the waiter counts the empty sticks and you are charged for those. I must say I wondered what happened to all the uneaten ones, but decided not to probe too deeply. The flavour was too good to spoil.

Finally, one must mention the hotels in Kuala Lumpur, of which there is now an abundance in the upper cost bracket. There are representatives from all the big chains, such as Hilton, Holiday Inn, and local ones such as Equatorial and Merlin. Neither hotels nor their restaurants are cheap, so the best way is to have a package costed before you leave home if possible. Quality is, however, very high, and in addition there are a lot of smaller, less expensive but equally comfortable places to choose from. The Station Hotel is still going strong, so is the Majestic, as are many others. I dislike recommending hotels because they can change in the time a book takes to be produced, and in any case people's tastes and pockets differ, but the Tourist Development Corporation of Malaysia produce a really comprehensive little directory of hotels in Malaysia and I would refer you to a perusal of that. The Corporation can, incidentally, supply literature on practically any happening in their country and have made great strides since their inception, as well as a considerable contribution to the industry which is becoming so very important to expanding Malaysia. If you want to avail yourself of their services on arrival go to their offices at Jalan Ampang, or ask one of the pretty and well informed girls in their kiosk at Subang airport. And that, after all, is where we came in.

4. South to the Causeway
Johore

For a newcomer to Malaysia, the road from Kuala Lumpur to
Seramban is almost exactly as he might expect it to be. In the
environs of Kuala Lumpur, tin mining is well in view, and
then come miles of rubber trees. They flash by in orderly rows,
separated occasionally by small kampongs where the wooden
houses roost on perches like quiet brown hens, and buffalo
stare impassively from their muddy waterholes. This quietly
rural landscape brings one into Negri Sembilan, whose name
means nine states. This refers to the group of Malay Chiefs
who ruled in this area. Seramban, its little capital, is about a
40 mile drive from K. L. and one afternoon I was thinking that
a cup of coffee wouldn't come amiss when as if he read my
thoughts, Saudi turned off the road and into the drive of the
Rest House. We climbed thankfully out of the car and into the
shaded interior of the building, and while we were waiting for
the coffee to appear, I was amused by a group of Indians who
were sitting around the little bar. Obviously lunch had been a
rather liquid affair and they were extremely happy, particularly one young, and very good-looking boy with a mop of
curly hair. I was told he was a Sikh and was surprised at the
lack of turban, but apparently many young Sikhs in Malaysia
are reluctant to adopt the traditional headgear now . . . in view
of the rumpus in Britain over crash helmets, I could see the
humour in the situation. . . . There was a slight pause in the
rendering of Indian songs when a large coach pulled up and a
bevy of Australian girls swarmed into the Rest House and in
search of the 'Ladies Room'. Then, louder than ever, came a
song . . . in English . . . which could have only been learned

from the knee of the British Army! ... the echoes of British rule come at strange moments. I don't know why Seramban Rest House supplies the best coffee in the area, but it does, and I'd recommend you stopping there when driving this route. You could have lunch if in time. It is reasonably priced and served immaculately. You can even have Gula Malacca for sweet ...! The Rest House is easy to find, because it is near the spectacular nine pillared mosque and the pleasant gardens.

Seramban is in the middle of an area which was settled long ago by West Sumatrans, and their influence can be seen in the type of house found there now. Particularly attractive is the State Museum. Originally the home of a prince in Ampang Tinggi, the building was brought to its present site and reconstructed piece by piece, and it has some particularly lovely examples of royal headdresses as well as a host of fearsome Dyak swords and ceremonial daggers. But the most unusual thing is the building itself with its magnificent attap roof, curved into twin horned ends, which give rise to its name, Minangkabau ... buffalo horns, and the beautifully carved wooden panels. This art is a vanishing one today. There is no longer the call for this type of work in the building of modern houses, so the woodcarvers turn their skills to furniture and home furnishings such as lampstands, salad bowls etc. Designs are traditional and you should particularly look for the cloud and flower patterns. You will, incidentally, find these same motifs is much Malay silverware.

From Seramban, the road goes to Port Dickson, and almost before you realise it, you are running alongside the sea. It is such a quiet sea, with hardly any 'salt smell', that one comes upon it almost by stealth, particularly if the tide is out, but you realise its presence by the numbers of small hostelries which cluster along its length, very popular as a holiday spot for Singaporeans. There are plenty of places to choose here, and you might be tempted to linger here rather than in K. L. if you've got a car, purely because of its holiday atmosphere, and it is cooler. Besides, it is only an hour or so from Malacca, and would make a good kicking off point for explorations there. This part of the coast is rich in history and you will remember that I told you that Tanjong Tuan was said to be the burial place of the founder and first ruler of Malacca. Not far from Port Dickson there is the tomb of a Sheikh, Ahmad Majnun, dated 1467 but near to it are some strange stones. No one knows exactly what they are, but they are thought to be Hindu in origin, or even perhaps, connected with sun worship in even earlier times. Tanjong Tuan is known also by its European name of Cape Rachado, and you can go to it by a steep and winding road, as far as its lighthouse, first placed there by the Portuguese to help their ships along the pirate-ridden Straits. 'Officially' the lighthouse is closed to visitors, but from its tower there is the most superb view on a clear day, across the Straits to far-off Sumatra. It is said that, long ago, Sumatra was joined to Tanjong Tuan by a narrow isthmus, but that it was destroyed by violent storms.

I thought on my latest sortie to Port Dickson that it had changed very little indeed over the years from the pleasant village it has always been, but I did think that prices, even with inflation, were high in comparison to K. L. Two fresh lime juice drinks, at Sri-Rusa, cost over £1. And this was not a luxury establishment, just a very pleasant seaside one. Two course lunch and coffee at Seramban would have only cost that. . . . It *is* necessary to look around a bit, if costs matter to you in Malaysia, but on the whole they are reasonable.

Godinho de Eredia, writing in 1613, said of his birthplace, 'This land (Malacca) is the freshest and most agreeable in the world. Its air is healthy and vivifying, good for human life and health, at once warm and moist, but neither the heat nor the moisture is excessive, for the heat is tempered by the moist vapours arising from the waters.'

Certainly the little breezes one encounters when driving into this, the most historic place in all the Malaysian Peninsular, are welcome, particularly after a long drive from K. L. or Singapore. Malacca . . . it is rather strange as one arrives in this sleepy, seedy looking town to realise that without its *raison d'être*, Malaysia itself might never have come into its present importance. Malacca's importance as a trading post, its strategic importance for the defence of craft plying the notorious Straits against pillage, piracy, murder and war, and its consequent shuttling back and forth among Portuguese, Dutch and British brought so much more of the Peninsula to the notice of the adventurers and merchants and indeed, Singapore itself owes its existence to Malacca's fame as a port, just as Malacca owed its previous life to the arrival of people from Singapura. Looking at Malacca at first glance today, one wouldn't give it a second as having anything to recommend it, except as an interesting little place with good antique shops. Then, the second glance is the one that counts. And another, and another until all the fascination and interest spreads around and over one until yesterday becomes more important than today, and stepping across the wooden doorstep of Cheng Hoon Temple is like walking through the Looking Glass.

This temple, in Jalan Kasjid, is the oldest Chinese Temple in Malaysia, and is dedicated to the colony who lived in Malacca at the time of the visit of Admiral Cheng Ho. The huge gates face on an unimpressive little shopping street, and a little Chinese man with a face like a withered apple waves one courteously inside towards the courtyard, into a mist of joss and burning offerings emanating from a potbellied stove in a further alcove. The temple itself has a rather dark interior, but as eyes grow accustomed to the gloom, one can see that the altars are beautifully inlaid with mother of pearl before brilliant images and their pillars are gilded. So too are the guardian lions, and like everyone else, I rubbed their heads for luck before leaving. Cheng Ho eventually became a deity to Chinese, and bears the religious title Sam Po, and in this temple, there is an inscription which records his visit to 'Bukit China'. This is the ancient cemetery behind the town, built on a hill as all Chinese cemeteries must be, partly to preserve the graves, but also to allow the spirits to overlook the happenings of the living. Bukit China is probably the oldest Chinese Cemetery in Malaysia, for it dates to the Ming Dynasty. In 1459 the Emperor sent his daughter, Princess Hong Lim Pa to marry Sultan Mansur Shah, and with her, he sent a court composed of 500 ladies of noble birth. They, of course, eventually married into local families, which was highly satisfactory to all concerned. The Sultan gave his Princess a hill 'without the town', and promised that the land would be theirs for all time. The ladies had a well built on 'Den China' (Siamese for Residence of Chinese) and legend has it that if a visitor drinks from the water, he will come again to Malacca before he dies. But, it is covered now with wire mesh against possible pollution, so I would advise not to push your luck!

The place which appears on every picture postcard of Malacca is the once elegantly spick and span buildings comprising the Stadhuys and clock tower, remnants of Dutch occupation. They are shabby now, red and white paint peeling, and the long staircase to the main building is dustily deserted on a Saturday afternoon when offices are closed. Christ Church too stands locked and silent, so let's walk another 200 yards along the road and find the Malacca Museum. This is the best place from which to start any exploration of Malacca, and is housed in an old Dutch building dating from about 1660. Once it was a private house belonging to expatriates from Holland, but in more recent times it was used as Government quarters by senior officers in the Public Works Department. It was made available as the Malacca Museum by General Sir Gerald Templar when he was High Commissioner of the Federation of Malaya in 1953, and it has a comprehensive coverage of the cultures which have been absorbed into Malacca over the centuries as well as much of Southern Peninsular Malaysia. It would be a pity to miss the museums in K. L. and Singapore, but should this be forced upon a visitor, then this little one could at least fill in some gaps and give a good idea of history, customs, and the way of life of yesterday and the day before. Almost the first thing one sees after entry is a painting showing the proclamation by the illustrious Envoy Cheng Ho (again!) and the presentation of the yellow dragon robe, the yellow umbrella and the jade seal, which signified the authority, in the Emperor's name, of the Sultan of Malacca. There are also interesting sketches of the town during the time of the Portuguese, which help a lot when going later to Santiago gate. During the first siege of Malacca by the Dutch, a certain De Jong recorded, that, of the 12,000 people living in Malacca only 600 survived and that he (de Jong) learned that 'Malacca was not the kind of cat to be taken without gloves'.

There are so many fragments of living collected together under the roof of the Malacca Museum. The house itself is an interesting one and must have been lovely when occupied as a residence. Its ceilings are high, the rooms very cool, and the old fans from Public Works days are still *in situ*. There are sketches of the Golden Age under Sultan Mansur Shah, Portuguese swords, Malay krisses, British swords, pictures of the British surrender, and the Japanese surrender, both of which have very large parts in Malaysia's historical past. Upstairs, I found a fine Dutch cupboard, drums and Portuguese uniforms of a type worn in the sixteenth century. These were presented by the Portuguese Government, for the originals could not have survived in Malacca's climate. There are flags, and a model of an early Portuguese ship similar to those which must have brought the first soldiers to Malacca. Incongruously alongside them, there is a picture of an aeroplane. This craft, apparently was sent to the First World War on 8th July 1916. It was called Malacca Chinese No.2 and was paid for 'by the Towkeys of Malacca'. Rather unfairly, it lists in meticulous fashion, the amounts subscribed by each Towkey. . . .

Among the Chinese furniture collection there are one or two magnificent pieces, inlaid with mother of pearl and intricately carved into dragons and lucky symbols. There is a bridal couch too. Narrow, wooden and with gold leafed carvings. It must have been jolly hard for the bride. . . . Another room is full of traditional Chinese wedding costumes with embroidered panels which are increasingly rare and costly today. There is also a collection of Malay wedding finery, complete with golden crowns and even a ceremonial throne and all items were decorated with crowns, ships and stars. Downstairs at the rear of the building is a small selection of Chinese porcelain, corals, and descriptions of padi (rice) fields, and in a courtyard is a whacking great crocodile. I'm uncertain where it came from, but it must have been from the nearby river. . . . Perhaps, in all the museum, the most incongruous thing was a notice. In Malay, Chinese and in English, it said 'Silence'. As the Museum was packed with Dutch tourists at the time, it wasn't a bit of use. But I guess Malacca is as much part of Dutch history as ours and the Malays, so I don't think it mattered greatly.

Under Albuquerque, the Portuguese built a large fortress at Malacca in 1511, but, after the eight months' siege by the Dutch in 1641, there was only a ruin left. Today there isn't even that. One archway only remains, called Santiago. It is as big as a small house, and is the haunt of postcard touts and souvenir sellers who stay within its shade while eating their rice from the usual paper cornet, as well as providing a picturesque background for local wedding groups – another activity which was taking place while I was there last time. The arch has some curlicues which remind one of Lisbon's Manoline architecture, and therefore of Portuguese power in past decades. I was told that a tunnel connects A. Famosa with St. John's hill. It is sealed now, but it proves just how vast and seemingly indestructible the fortifications once were. And, there is St. Paul's.

It is a steep walk to the top of the hill, but the view across Malacca and the Strait hasn't changed since this old church was built from laterite in 1521. It is in ruins now, but it was erected in gratitude to our Lady of Grace, for the deliverance of Portuguese sailors from the wrath of the sea. The Eastern Saint, St. Francis Xavier, preached within its walls, and when he died in 1553, he was buried there for a while before his body was removed to Goa. His empty tomb is still there, surrounded by a small rail. When Malacca fell to the Dutch, the Church was renamed St. Paul's, but with the building of Christ Church in 1753 from bricks brought all the way from Middleburg in Holland, the Portuguese building was allowed to fall into disrepair. It was of course, still hallowed ground, so the Dutch used it as a burial place for the more important personages in the Colony. Their tombstones are placed around the walls now, and they have a strange 'photographed' look about them, as if they are not quite real. Most bear names unknown, except to their once loved ones, but one slab echoes across the world to another continent. It marks the grave of Frau van Riebeck, wife of Jan van Riebeck, founder of the Cape Colony. The original stone was removed to Cape Town in 1915, but the mortal remains of the wife of the man forever connected with Dutch colonisation of South Africa are buried here, thousands of miles from her home in Holland and from her husband's New World.

A few yards from the church ruins, looking out across the town, is a statue of St. Francis Xavier. It is in white stone, but one of the arms is missing from the elbow downwards. I was told a strange tale about this statue by someone who bears a Portuguese name and is of a Catholic family, but who is unmistakably of Tamil descent so that the blood, somewhere long ago, was mixed. . . . And as her soft voice related the story as it had been told to her, I felt that it might, just possibly, be true. . . .

When it came to the time that the body of St. Francis Xavier was to be disinterred in readiness for reburial in Goa, it was found to be in very good condition – almost a miracle in a climate where decay is very rapid. The people were anxious for the Pope to canonise their good man, so they cut off the right arm of the corpse at the elbow, and sent it to Rome to prove its condition, and, in due course, they received permission for the Saint to be recognised. Some time later, it was decided to erect a statue to the Saint outside this church where he had preached, and this was duly carried out. Naturally, he was depicted as a whole man, as he had been in life, but on the day it was erected, a wind arose, blowing down a tree. It fell across the statue and removed the right arm . . . at the elbow.

There is another delightful story about St. Francis which bears repeating, and which is better known than the first one. The Saint was walking along the beach at Malacca one day, with his rosary in his hand, when he dropped it into the sand. Despite diligent searching, it had disappeared completely and this distressed St. Francis very much. He prayed that despite the impossibility of finding anything in the sand, a miracle might happen and that his rosary would be restored to him, and then he walked further along the beach. Coming towards him was a crab, and upon its back, it bore the lost rosary. St. Francis bent down, took up the rosary from the shell of the crab, and blessed the creature, making the sign of the Cross over it. To this day, there is one species of crab in Malaysia which bears a cross upon its back, and occasionally the fisherman find it in their nets. Look for it in the fishmarkets.

There is another echo of Portuguese occupation. More lasting perhaps than any of the others, but quieter. . . . This is the community which, to this day, lives in the small, humble houses, almost identical one to another, in the Portuguese Eurasian Settlement. The homes would appear hardly to have altered over the years and stand along roads which bear the names of the past, such as Albuquerque. There is poverty there, standpipes provide the running water, they are the sort of houses which, if seen in settlements in South Africa, would be loudly condemned as unsuitable . . . but there are television aerials, motorbikes and not a few nice cars. Most of the folk who dwell there take their living from the sea. All are Catholic, and all are very proud indeed of their history. They have every right to be. It is a long and honoured one.

On the way back from the Settlement I stopped off to look at St. John's Fort, plodding up the steep path from the road as many a British solider must have done, for this is one of the only fortified places that the British upheld in Malacca when they swopped Bencoolen, in Sumatra, with the Dutch for the Malaysian colony. The thick walls are still there, showing that it must have been impressive once in its guardianship of the Strait, but now there is little to see and the fort is overlooked by a watertower and a block of flats, almost losing its identity . . . almost . . . until one remembers that it was here that a Siamese Buddhist statue was found. The statue was placed in Malacca museum, but, how did it get there . . . and when . . . and why? There are many such questions in Malacca, but the dead don't give up their secrets easily to the curious, particularly to the ones with only an afternoon to spare. Dead or alive, Malacca and Malaccans take their time. There are, at the time of writing, some plans by an Italian company to establish a tourist complex on Pulau Besar, an island off the Malaccan coast. It envisages chalets, shops, restaurant and even a hydrofoil service back and forth to the mainland. It could be the kiss which would waken this one time Beauty from her long sleep. Anything can happen in Malacca. It has ... in her past. ...

The road southward resolves itself into a comfortably rolling progress. Endless vistas of oil palms, bananas, pineapples and the ever-present rubber, small brown kampongs dozing under coconut palms where a suspended line of flapping batik sarongs proclaim an indecipherable message. Sometimes one sees a pair of bullocks plodding solidly in front of the curved Malaccan carts, though these are not nearly so numerous as they used to be. Time was when every bend had its own bullock cart hazard. Now it is usually an overloaded and elderly small van, or an open-backed lorry with a dozen or so impassive bluecoated farmworkers jolting homewards to the little towns. Under the Emergency, these were stopped at the high fences into these same towns and searched. Now, as we still roll through the main streets of the towns, the radios blare from each openfronted shophouse, each on a different channel according to the race living there, and there is little else to disturb the peace. May it stay that way, for it was hard earned. ... These kampongs and towns were not always peaceful, even before the ugly days of the Emergency. There were always the dangers of pirate raids along the coast, and at Kampong Parid Pechar, just about 16 miles from Muar, there is a graveyard with 99 tombstones. The legend tells that at a wedding festival, a lovesick swain, crazed with jealousy at the sight of his beloved marrying another, plunged his spear into the unfortunate bridegroom. Not content with that, he then withdrew the weapon and polished off the rest of the village one by one, including the bride. What they were all doing to let him accomplish all that singlehanded, we aren't told ... but the graves have been there for 500 years and the story has remained constant. This main road from Singapore to K. L. was a joy to me when I travelled it first, used as I had been all my life to the congested highways of London and the Home Counties. Today, there is a considerable increase in traffic density, but it is hardly to be placed in motorway category and one gets a great deal of pleasure from driving its well engineered surfaces. However, do be alert for the sudden and unannounced arrival in front of you of some plantation lorry lurching from a gateway. They have been doing it for years and the extra tourist traffic really doesn't account for much against habits of a lifetime.

At Muar, a bridge has taken the place of the ancient ferry so one doesn't take a welcome break any more while the car wobbles its way across the brown waters on the groaning planks. But the kids still splash in the shallows and one longs to join them. Onward though, and the country opens up now, giving glimpses of mountains and fields. This is a lovely land where the ridges of hills are often wisped by small clouds. You will see Mount Ophir, known in Malay as Gunong Ledang. Some say that the mountain houses a fairy princess. Others that all men who see her must fall in love with her. I think it is the mountain itself which casts the spell, for once in love with Malaysia, it is a permanent affection. Godinho, that fount of knowledge on sixteenth century Malacca and district recorded that the aborigines dwelt there. They were known as Orang Benua, and they were sorcerers who transformed themselves into tigers to prey upon the unfortunate Malaccans. But, when the Bishop solemnly excommunicated the tigers in a service of High Mass, they never came again. Such is the material of history and legend of which all Malaysia is made. . . .

Inland from Batu Pahat is Kluang, almost central in the great State of Johore, through which you are now passing. The second richest area in the state, after the capital, Johore Bahru, and named after the flying fox (keluang) it is not particularly interesting for the historically minded tourist, but it is the place to look at if requiring to see some of the industrial development which has come directly from Kluang's position in the centre of considerable agricultural wealth. It is a pleasant town now, and perhaps for someone who reads this, it will bring nostalgic memories as a Squadron station for the Royal Air Force. . . . Back along the coast road and down to Kukup. This ramshackle little village has an important place in Johore, but it isn't for its beauty or its history. It is the best place to eat Chili Crabs. Be prepared to sit down at rickety old tables on the planked walks above the sea, and eat until you can eat no more, as you eat the crabs with your fingers, *don't* wear your best dress. If you are allergic to sea food, don't worry, they'll find you something else. But in that case my heartfelt sympathies are yours for the treat you'll miss.

The State of Johore has always been among the most progressive as well as the wealthiest in all Malaysia. Its history is a long one. It was from the Sultan of Johore and his Temenggong that Britain obtained the concession on Sinagapore, but again we have to look back before that time. Certainly there were civilisations along the banks of the Johore River over a thousand years ago, and it is also said that that same river is the one described by Ptolemy as the 'Palanda's' when he referred to the Golden Chersonese. But in times nearer to our own, Johore as we know it today, began when the Portuguese attacked Malacca in 1511. The ruling Sultan of Malacca fled from the onslaught with others of his house, to set up again along the banks of Johore River. At that period, Johore consisted of Pahang, Riau (Rhio) Johore and Singapore and Lingga where the titular head lived. There has always been some argument on whether Sultan Husain and his Temenggong had the right to cede Singapore to Sir Stamford Raffles. Husain died in Malacca and was succeeded by Sultan Ali, and in 1855 he in turn ceded the sovereignty of Johore to Temenggong Daing Ibrahim, the great grandfather of the present Sultan. At that time the capital was at Johore Lama, and little more than a village. The new Sultan moved the capital to Johore Bahru, just across from Singapore island where he had been living in Telok Belanga. However, before he could do much more, he died, leaving his son, Abu Bakar, as Sultan in his stead.

Sultan Abu Bakar built the Istana in Johore Bahru, encouraged clearance and cultivation of former jungle land, widened rivers, and improved Johore's trade by using Singapore as a ready made market. He travelled widely in Europe too, even coming to Britain to see Queen Victoria, who apparently took a great liking to the personable prince. She created the title of Maharajah for him in 1868, and remember that, at this time, there was *no* British Resident, so the title was a present from one ruler to another. The Sultan also encouraged friendship with the East, too, welcoming Chinese settlers in large numbers and, as a result, in 1892 he received the First Class Order of the Dragon from the Emperor of China. But, by far the most important achievement of Sultan Abu Bakar as far as his people were concerned was his establishment of a written constitution by which the State has been ruled ever since, and which proved to be the foundation stone upon which his State advanced towards prosperity at a far greater rate than any of the others. When his son succeeded to the throne in 1895, he continued the advancement of people and state, in particular by introducing a railway line.He borrowed ten million from the Federated Malay States Government with which to build it. It was extremely fortunate for him that the rubber boom coincided with the opening of the line. Sultan Ibrahim implemented the constitution even further by inserting a clause which reads 'The Sultan is not truly a ruler whose will and pleasure rules and not the law.' A revolutionary step for an autocratic Malay Prince. Judiciary, education and health and road systems followed during the years, particularly after the British Adviser was appointed in 1914, and prosperity seemed assured. The Second World War, and the Emergency which followed so closely, caused many difficult and heartbreaking incidents, but Johore survived and today is still one of the most prosperous States in Malaysia. It exports rubber, copra, pineapples, palm oil, sago, tapioca and of course there are still spices, for gambier and pepper were always main crops over the years. Mining is important, and in local agriculture there have been great advances. Poultry is farmed in quantity now and Australian dairy cattle arrived on a large farm in Johore in 1976. We have to see how they will fare. But a big and coming industry is tourism, for this state is so near crowded Singapore that it cannot fail to attract holidaymakers from there in large numbers, particularly day trippers, so income will be substantial. Johore Bahru, set as it is alongside the Strait, still occasionally manages to retain a certain 'rustic' atmosphere, despite the new flyover and the multi-storey complex. The new Customs complex should, by the time this book is in print, be in full operation and by removing the endless stream of lorries from the centre of the town, it will bring sighs of relief from the beleaguered townspeople. There aren't many hotels yet, probably because most visitors are passing through on their way to somewhere else, but there are plenty of small cafes, restaurants, discos, etc, as well as a cinema or two which show films banned (surprisingly) in nearby, sometimes puritanical, Singapore. For the sightseer, there is the Abu Bakar mosque, named after the Sultan who put the State on its road to modernity, and who was the grandfather of the present Sultan Ismail. The Sultan's Palace, known as Istana Besar, is open every morning except on Fridays and Public Holidays, but even so, make prior arrangements with the Controller of the Royal Household. (The private Palace Bukit Serene, is *not* open to the public.) There is a Zoo in the Palace Grounds. I have never liked animals to be kept in close captivity, so I really cannot enthuse about this place at all.

Much pleasanter in my eyes is a trip to Kota Tinggi, and nine miles onward from the little town, the beautiful waterfalls. There is safe bathing in the pools but be warned that the water is very cold in comparison to the warmth of the air around you, so don't catch a chill. There is a pleasant little restaurant facing the falls, as well as a few small chalets which can be reserved in advance for an overnight stay. This is an idea if wishing to take a trip down river to the old site of the capital, at Johore Lama. At the time of writing there are ambitious plans afoot to build new hotels and restaurants at Tanjong Penawar. Day facilities will hopefully be open in late 1976, so it might be an idea to visit the area in any case if looking for an excursion without too much effort, but it will be at least 1978 before the main projects are completed. There is at present, considerable interest from overseas investment, so it could be a very profitable project indeed.

One of my favourite excursions when living in Singapore, was always towards Mersing. I still think that this particular part of Malaysia remains among the most attractive for the tourist with a day or more to spare on excursions from the Lion City, but things have changed. You must now get a car permit if driving from Singapore and this can be obtained at J Holland Park, not far from 'Tourist City', and you must also remember to take your passport. The enlightened times when these were not necessary between Singapore and Malaysia have unfortunately disappeared for the time being. If you want to go by bus, it leaves at nine a.m. daily from Taufik Travel Service, Bussorah Street, Singapore.

Beyond Kota Tinggi the road runs once again through miles of rubber plantations and jungle where a wild pig might run squealing across the road, narrowly missing your wheels. Although this road is used a great deal by day trippers from Singapore it still retains a mainly rural aspect, and it isn't difficult to imagine how it must have been when the Japanese rode their bicycles down this self same road to attack an unsuspecting and careless Singapore. There is a signpost, somewhere about 58 miles from Johore Bahru, which points down a side road. It simply says Telok Mahkota. It used to say Jason's Bay, which is exactly the same place, and which has one of the nicest stretches of beach anywhere in the Southern Malaysian Peninsula. There isn't much else except the beach and palm-tree or two which provide a very small amount of shade, but it is a heavenly spot if you can take a lot of sunshine. I spent a happy afternoon there, spoiling the siesta of dozens of indignant little crabs so that they scuttled back to the safety of the shallow warm waters, disappearing below the sand far from the reach of my enquiring rubber sandal. I paid for it that night with an overdose of sunburn, a rare occurrence for a leatherback like me, so be aware that the sun can be very dangerous in combination with calm blue seas and a softly deceptive breeze.

Mersing itself is little more than a village, though it

possesses a Government Rest House and several small hotels. Its main claim to fame is that one can hire a boat there, and it is the only place from which one can get by water transport to Bali Hai. Be easy, we are still in the South China Sea, not the South Pacific. It is just that, when the movie moguls were searching for a location in which to photograph the famous James Michener story, they were lucky enough to find Pulau Tioman, some 30 or so miles off the East Coast of Malaysia, and as any one who saw the movie can vouch, it was the perfect setting they required. The island is pearshaped and has two mountain peaks, known as the Asses Ears, which for generations have been landmarks for sailors. Even the Arab traders called for freshwater, and it is rumoured that, hidden in the mountains are treasures from the Ming Dynasty left by Chinese sailors, though so far nothing has been discovered. Fresh water supplies are still excellent which is one of the reasons why the present developments are possible, for, after being thus thrust into the twentieth century, it was unthinkable to many that this paradise should ever revert to its pristine state, when there were only four small villages and a total of two thousand fisherfolk. Pahang State Development Corporation (the island belongs to Pahang though only acceessible by sea from Mersing in Johore) started to 'develop' it. At the moment only the first phase has been completed, so the time to go there is, without doubt, now, because the combination of modern Merlin hotel and untouched Garden of Eden is a formidable one. All the sunlit days can be spent in the magical watery world of the skindiver and the snorkeller, or in the mysterious hinterland of the island, evenings bring the opportunity to dine in an hotel which has all the comforts of its sisters in Kuala Lumpur, Panang or Kuantan, and then listen to the sheer enchantment of a tropical night which, even here, miles from the main stream of civilisation is anything but silent, though the 'noise' comes from the sea, insistent upon the sand, washing away every trace of daytime footprints, and from the legsong produced by the millions of crickets. I don't think this paradise can possibly last. All too soon the second and third phases of the Development plans will be carried out and more holidaymakers will inevitably find their way by air and boat to Pulau Tioman, bringing the three death knells to peace and quiet . . . tape recorders, transistors and television, in active and constant use. But . . . and this is important . . . it will enable a great many more people to enjoy the pleasures of an earthly paradise than hitherto have been possible, and that after all is 'progress', or the price of it.

At Rawa, only ten miles from Mersing, there are also chalets for hire, but most of the many other islands in the area are uninhabited, or have a small community of fisherpeople who are sometimes willing to act as guides to enthusiastic reef explorers. To get to these islands, it is necessary to hire a boat and you could sleep on board, or on the beach. Either way, it isn't too comfortable. The boats, as I have already indicated have to be obtained from Mersing, and in all probability the Boatmen's Association would come to some amicable arrangement, but it isn't a very cheap pastime. Still I suppose Paradise itself won't come as cheap as all that if we are ever privileged enough to get there. In the meantime, this could make a very satisfactory substitute.

5. Looking East

Thunder had raged all night around K. L., accompanied by spectacular displays of lightning, both sheet and forked, and by driving rainstorms which fell, like steel-rodded curtains, until gurgling recklessly into monsoon drains. I'd been riveted to the balcony for some of the night, watching the Brock's Benefit, and in consequence was a little heavy-eyed as I waited on the steps of the Merlin Hotel in the early dawn for my car and my Malaysian companions to arrive. But morning was fresh and sweet, coming with a newly washed face and a gentle touch, and I soon forgot my slight weariness as we set out, in the clear grey light, for part of the charm of the East is in these tremendous changes in Nature's moods. After leaving the untidier outskirts of K. L., past the rubber factory, and the turn-off to the Batu Caves, the road climbs, gently and inexorably towards the Genting Highlands, looking down over wide, tree-filled valleys, running through deep forests where thick ropes of liana hang from the tall trees, and the rivers, thick and brown like milk chocolate or the 'cafe su-su' so beloved by Malaysians, wind between sharp banks beside small villages, which are indistinguishable one from another to a newcomer's eye, yet each with its own life awaking slowly in the soft air.

The whole of Malaysia finds its way around by the meticulously placed milestones, a legacy from British days, and directions usually include such phrases as 'so and so' house, just past such and such milestone'. Nowadays, the term 'Batu' which is Malay for stone, is being used increasing-

ly as well as the changeover to kilometres, but old habits die
hard, and the ubiquitous milestone is a most comforting companion wherever one travels. Genting Highlands is 32 miles
from K. L., climbing steadily to peaks of nearly 4000 feet,
and it is in this setting that a smart casino has been installed
for the pleasure of K. L. citizens and the steady stream of
would-be gamblers who come along the excellent highway
from Singapore. There is a large and luxurious hotel for them
all to stay in, with some of the most magnificent views in
Malaysia on a good day. This might be the place also to mention Cameron Highlands and Fraser's Hill, both exceedingly
valuable as local vacation centres, for they act as lungs for the
people who live in the hot humidity of the lower altitudes.
These highland resorts were originally established by the
British for the use of expatriates on short leave to avoid the
long and expensive sea journey back to Europe for personnel
needing a break from the very trying conditions then prevalent in tropical climates. Remember air-conditioning and
preventive tropical medicine are both comparatively recent innovations. Writing in 1906, Sir Frank Swettenham commented, 'In the centre of the main range of Malay hills there
are about 100,000 acres of undulating country at a height
of 4000 feet, and it is probable that in time, a large station
may be established there, more especially if planters find
that the soil is suitable for profitable cultivation. The
highland referred to, originally explored by Mr. W. Cameron
under Government auspices, is less than 40 miles from a
point on the Perak trunk railway.' William Cameron had
reported in 1885 that there was a 'fine plateau with gentle
slopes shut in by lofty mountains', and his investigations obviously proved invaluable. Tea plantations were set up,
Chinese market gardeners arrived, and nowadays all the excellent produce is found throughout Malaysia.

Fraser's Hill, about 60 miles from Kuala Lumpur, was only
established after the First World War, and there is an amusing story told about it. At the beginning of that war, Bishop
Ferguson Davie of Singapore thought that he ought to find
that Briton, a mule train operator, called Fraser, who lived

somewhere in the heights beyond the Gap, marking the Selangor/Pahang border, to tell him about the terrible happenings in Europe. The good prelate, accompanied by a constable, struggled all the way up to the summit of the hill, only to find that the Briton had fled on knowing that the Law was on its way. He had very good reason, for the area was nothing more than a gambling and opium den. Fraser was never seen again, but his name lives on in the delightful resort which now covers seven hills. British visitors find these hill resorts have a most familiar aspect, for many of the houses look as if they have been imported directly from English suburban settings, stockbrokers' Tudor and all, and roses, marigolds and delphiniums grow side by side with frangipani and orchids, bearing mute witness to the loving ministration of generations of expatriates to whom the cool highlands assuaged the pangs of homesickness, and for whom the great treat was to light a fire in the living rooms of the hill bungalows and pretend that they were 'home' . . . . I know how it was, for I was one of them.

The road from the Gap Rest House to Fraser's Hill is winding and very narrow and is controlled by gates, open at odd hours, for 30 minutes at a time. Once is counted through at each end, as a safety measure. On the many occasions I have driven this road, there have always been large monkeys swinging in the trees near the road, and we had to shut the car windows as a safety precaution. A pity, when, for the first time, one suddenly discovers that the band of sweat around one's middle has disappeared and the air is as cool as a summer day in Scotland.

Both Cameron Highlands and Fraser's Hill have undergone a measure of facelift since Colonial days, with several large hotels making their appearance alongside the bungalows and rest houses and in consequence, the golf course, swimming pools and beautiful walks are very well patronised, particularly at weekends and there is no longer the complete tranquillity that once prevailed. But they are lovely places to run away to, when the climate of Singapore or Kuala Lumpur gets the better of one, as it can on constant acquaintance, and their future in the domestic holiday map of Malaysia is assured. Incidentally, it was on the Fraser's Hill Road, during the Emergency, that the ambush occurred of Sir Henry Gurney, High Commissioner to Malaya. On the 7th October 1951, Sir Henry and his wife, his secretary and chauffeur, were travelling in the car towards the hill station when the insurgents opened fire. Sir Henry got out of the car, presumably to draw the fire from his wife, and he was hit, and died at the roadside. The spot is marked. Today, with the threat of Communism again raising its head in South-East Asia, the Malaysian Government is faced with terrorists in some areas, more particularly along the border with Thailand, where Chin Peng lives out his bitterness in the jungle deeps. Pahang too has some problems, poised like a dagger towards Malaysia's heart. But the Government is firm in its resolve to deal with the threat to their peace and will surely use the same relentlessness as the British did in the fifties. Let us hope that they are rewarded with the same success, for otherwise, this lovely gentle land would bleed to death from its wounds.

Pahang! The largest and to my mind the most excitingly different state in Peninsular Malaysia. It remains almost completely unspoiled and this is in part due to the nature of its terrain. As we have already remarked, the mountain ranges slope far more gently towards the East Coast, and the jungles have had an opportunity to grow luxuriantly, supplying excellent and very beautiful hardwoods, much prized both in the domestic and export markets. But the mountain ranges were not the only reason for the comparative disuse of the East Coast. The north-east monsoon is prevalent upon its shores from October to April and for centuries has restricted ship movement. Particularly was this so with the advent of steamers, for the river entrances were mostly blocked with sandbars, and in consequence what traffic there was, went more to Siam, who in any case retained more influence over the States affected. One sees this influence still in their customs and in their way of life. At the present time, work is proceeding on the construction of a new harbour just north of Kuantan which, when completed, will inevitably change the face of the East Coast beyond recognition. Until then, we may selfishly continue to enjoy the unsophisticated and still isolated area to the full. In addition to all this there is but one road from Kuala Lumpur which is used by all the commercial traffic and it is a long hot drive. Hence my early start. In spite of it, there was a surprising amount of local vehicles, all of them intent on staying in the middle of the road with varied cargoes of livestock, rubber, canned pineapple, and one, loaded to the gunwales with toilet rolls of every hue. Each vehicle was a major obstacle when combined with the sinuous bends of the mountain stretch. A short distance past the turn-off to the Genting Highlands, near Bentong, there were several small fruit stalls by the roadside, selling local produce. I bought the very small sweet bananas which taste so much better than the huge ones we get in Britain, custard apples, the small oranges we know as mandarins (which are not grown in Malaysia but imported from China) and half a kilo of root ginger. We can of course get the latter in Britain, but in spite of the effort of carrying the root all round Malaysia with me, I get an extra thrill when adding its delicate flavour to dishes here at home, and always, I am back on a fragrantly warm morning in the heart of Malaysia's green and pleasant land.

There is a nice little Rest House at Bentong where one gets good coffee, but I was anxious to get a little further, and pushed on to Temerloh. The Rest House there is an airy pleasant building where one can also get coffee, or a meal. I plumped for the former. Jane, a petite Indian girl, who has one of the healthiest appetites I've ever met, chose fried rice, and when I saw it I wished I'd joined her, but it was time to move on again. Temerloh itself is a quiet town enlivened only at weekends by the market near the mosque, which is incidentally a rather attractive one. The market is usually a purely local affair with yams, coconuts and bamboo shoots etc., brought in by small boats from the surrounding villages along the Pahang River. One can get on one of these boats and travel to Pekan the royal capital, stopping at the villages en route. These communities are long established, for they came into being as trading places for the merchants from China and India who came in search, centuries ago, of the gold and tin known even then to be in the vicinity. Nowadays, most of the villagers are rubber tappers and padi planters.

Another excursion, using the Rest House as a base, is to adventure, again by boat, to Bera Lake, right in the heart of the Pahang jungle. Adventure is the right word . . . you'll have to camp out, taking all your supplies with you from Temerloh, but it's worth every moment of discomfort and heat to experience the atmosphere of Tasak Bera. You might, or might not, meet a tiger. This is the area for them and lookout has to be kept. And you shouldn't attempt to cool off in the lake, or the crocodiles might get a bigger breakfast than usual. I cannot speak from experience of this particular trip but I have taken similar ones, and in my opinion, any opportunity to look at the wilderness at close quarters is worth while. For those with sufficient time to spare, Taman Negara, the National Park, is bound to be a highlight in any Malaysian journey. There are camping facilities and specially built hides near the natural salt licks which attract the bigger game. For the less adventurous or the less able, there are small bungalows available as well as a Rest House at Kuala Tahan. This Rest House is also the administrative centre of the park and the powers that be have constructed an artificial salt lick near the premises. A variety of the smaller animals such as selandang, tapir and deer, seem to have mastered their distrust of humanity sufficiently to condescend to come there.

Rather more strenuous is the journey to be made up to the peak of Gunung Tahan, the highest peak in West Malaysia, or a penetration further into the jungle depths. Guides and porters are available for quite modest fees. I don't think I'd be prepared to walk those trails for the equivalent of £1.50 a day. But of course expenses don't end there. One has to get to Kuala Tembeling, or to the Jerantut Ferry. Then there is the coast of Hostel and/or Rest House, lodge, tent etc. hides, boats in the park area, photographic and fishing licences. I would advise anyone proposing to do this type of journey to write directly to the Chief Game Warden, Bangunan Maba (Tingkat 4) Jalan Davidson, Kuala Lumpur, and get the right advice for their exact requirements. With the time and money available it is worth every penny despite the leeches!

The road to Kuantan from Jerantut goes via Maran through jungle, past padifields where water buffalows wallow, through villages and pineapple and palm oil plantations. The latter is rapidly overtaking rubber as a valuable crop. The main drawback lies in the amount of space it requires but prices are good and demand for its legion products very high. In addition it is an attractive tree with its crown of fringes and its bunch of brown nutlike fruits. From the air, it always reminds me of the succulents one grows on rockgardens, but on close inspection it has tall sturdy growth, providing cool shade among the avenues in the heat of the day. The Jerantut/Maran road is a narrow one, timber lorries shoot out like jack-in-the-boxes from plantations and, in monsoon season, usually between November and January, the road may be flooded, with the additional hazard of fallen trees. Otherwise it is perfectly drivable.

South of Kuantan, the road goes to Mersing. Here, we will venture as far as Pekan, whose claim to fame is that it is Royal. The Sultan lives there in a modern Istana, and the best time to visit (if you aren't among the exalted who may have been invited to the recent Royal Wedding) is at the end of May. Then, the Sultan celebrates his Birthday (I think it is an official one) and for three days, the town is en fete. Wayang, Rodat, Orang Asli dances, Joget and of course presentations by the Chinese and Indian communities all take place in the grounds of the Istana Kota Beram, near the Police Station. But the undoubted highlight is the Fish Drive and this has to be seen to be believed. Just before the great day, tons of tuba roots are smashed into pulp to extract the juice. On the morning of the Drive, this juice is poured into the river waters upon which the Sultan, his guests and hundreds of his faithful subjects wait in small boats. The fish are intoxicated by the juice, float to the surface and are collected by the populace before the enforced drunkenness has time to wear off! It seems a high price for the poor fish to pay for a hangover, but that has been the way of things for quite a time in Pekan.

By the time we had completed the five hour drive from K. L. to Kuantan (it takes an hour by air) the heat was beginning to build up, clothes were soaking with sweat, and lunch and a cold drink seemed an excellent idea. The best place to find a reasonably priced lunch is in the tiny open air restaurants near the bus station and market. Don't be afraid to use these humble establishments anywhere in Malaysia and Singapore. There are no trimmings, no finesse, but food is fresh. If you follow custom and eat early, it will also be hot, but otherwise food is seldom served as hot as we are accustomed to in European countries. There is no need to worry about drinking the water. It is safe. There are plenty of alternatives, including the local beer, fruit juices etc, as well as good iced tea and coffee, and of course there's always a coconut. . . .

We set out after lunch in search of the said coconut. Not that there aren't plenty to be purchased in the market, but I wanted mine straight from the tree. As the trees are on the tall side and I'm not too fond of heights, I wanted someone else to shin up and get a nice ripe green nut for me. Who else but a monkey? This is not as simple as it seems. A baboon is the best, for this species has been trained to the job for centuries, but there aren't many of them around. We drove some kilometres out of Kuantan to Sungei Karang Darat, and stopped by an openfronted shophouse set beside a clump of coconut palms. But it was neither of these that caught my eye. It was the notice. Faded until almost unreadable it said, in Malay and English. . . . 'Coconut plucking by a baboon'. . . . Quite the nicest tourist sign I ever read!

Sure enough, in a few minutes a lean Malay, whose age could have been anything between 30 and 50 (it's difficult to tell age in Malaysia) appeared with a large baboon trotting like a dog on a leash beside him. A word from its master, and it started up the sloping trunk of the nearest palm, the Malay playing out the long rope as it climbed higher. At the top it stopped, and carefully examined several husks before selecting two and throwing them earthwards while we kept well out of the target area. The Malay tugged gently at the rope and the baboon scampered quickly down the tree, stood on its back legs as if to receive its applause, and bobbing and chattering in approval when we all obliged. I started forward a little to take a closer picture but he bared his teeth, so I kept my distance.

The big green-brown husks were opened with a few blows of a parang, and the slightly opaque, sweetish milk poured into glasses for us. It is one of the most pleasant and refreshing drinks in the world. The meat of the new nuts is soft, quite unlike the tough old things in circus coconut shies, and one scrapes it out with a spoon. I left a large amount in mine, not because I didn't like it, but because I wanted to present it to the baboon for his trouble. The last I saw of him as I drove away was a furry brown heap busily engaged in polishing off the last delicious morsels. I came across several other baboons in Malaysia whose main occupation was coconut picking, though not for the tourist trade, and they were all inclined to be crosspatches. I suppose I'd be the same way if I was sent up and down coconut palms for my living.

My next stops were to be at villages which have taken up small cottage industries at the behest of Kuantan's lively Tourist Officer, and for the next hour or two I bumped over cart tracks towards small kampongs crouched on the dusty ochre earth, beside some of fairest beaches along the East Coast. I longed to sidetrack into the milkywarm sea, but the villagers were expecting me and had promised to show their work, so there was no escape. To be fair, I didn't really want to run away, just to dally a little. The villages were sleepy in the afternoon sun, for most of the elders keep out of the heat and the only external sign of life as I walked in the shade afforded by the wooden stilted cottages were a few chickens, a young sarong clad girl, taking her bath in a corrugated iron enclosure reminiscent of a French pissoir, and a group of half-naked children. Their main activity was directed at trying to kill off some of the bats, roosting in the palms above, by stoning them. A couple of pathetic little bodies lay around, and I scolded in my halting Malay, using the words remembered from long ago when my own small daughter had got into mischief with Malay friends. It worked, particularly when I sidetracked attention to my camera, but it was probably only a very temporary measure. One cannot play God for long.

The villagers of Sungei Karang Darat are encouraged to make pretty souvenirs from the shells and driftwood found on the beaches. I watched them working in their 'factory', a small wooden building built like the rest of the village on stilts, and financed by local authority. Seated at two long tables, with a tube of Bostick and a candle over which to heat it, they fastened shells together into little birds and tortoises, dotting eyes and mouths with the black goo, and finally sitting the little creatures on driftwood perches or within small shell gardens. They were quite entrancing but impossible to carry across the world without mishap, so I left them to be sold in the Crafts Shop in Kuantan. This is run by the Tourist Office to meet the constant tourist demand. Orang Asli provide effective and reasonably priced carvings for the shop, so do dollmakers, songket workers, Mengkuang weavers . . . but I'm going too fast. All of them draw small supplementary incomes from this work. Nothing very big, but a few dollars is all one needs when the climate supplies the heating, the sea and the land provide the food, and clothing is but a sarong, washed at the village well and dried in an hour in the hot sun. The great thing as far as I was concerned in all these kampongs was the completely natural atmosphere in which all these little activities take place. The kampongs have been there for generations and their people take part in their small contribution to tourism as an extension of their everyday activities and not as an entire way of life. Indeed, their own lives come first, as I saw clearly for myself. I was welcomed everywhere into houses as an honoured guest, as I removed my shoes before crossing the threshold and ushered to the best of the few chairs, but while refreshment was being pressed upon me, one member of the family had been despatched to find the performers, and I was lucky if they happened to be around. For instance, the Bersilat performers, were all fishermen and had quite naturally gone to sea and wouldn't be back until next day. I arrived to see gasing, that is topspinning, a traditional sport on the East Coast, just as dusk fell. I was greeted with great courtesy and ushered in to watch television. It was a cowboy epic and I sat patiently with an assortment of entranced children, watching the antics of Smith and Jones in the velvety night. I could think of nothing more incongruous. . . . Then came a message that one of the demonstrators had a headache and wouldn't be coming, and he apparently was the key man. So we had hot sweet coffee, while the television vied with the noise of the crickets and the far off sound of the sea. Such is the charm of the East Coast.

While in the Kuantan area, I had hoped to stay at the Merlin Beach Hotel at Telok Chempedak so that I could be within sight of the South China Sea, and leave my verandah door open to the moist cool air, but it was not to be. Apparently one must book at least a month ahead at Merlin, limited as it is to a very few rooms. But it is being extended, so that the position will improve, and I shall look forward to going there then. Other hotels are also being built at this Beach, including a Hyatt, so there will be more choice as this pretty resort is developed, and there is no doubt that the requirement is there. Within Kuantan there are a number of 'Chinese' hotels, more suited to local business traffic. I make this distinction, not out of snobbery or any sort of criticism, but because they would not necessarily appeal to European tastes in decor etc. The exception might be the Samudra in the centre of the town, whose pleasant rooms at the rear of the hotel overlook the sluggish brown waters of the river. But it is quite a long way from the beaches and these, after all, are the magnet on this coast. As far as I am concerned, the main drawback with all the hotels I stayed in with the exception of the Merlins at Penang and K. L. was the noisy air-conditioning. I much preferred the old days when one relied on fresh air and mosquito nets, but now one's eardrums are assailed by the rushing noise of the very effective cooling plants. I'm not alone in this dislike. I met a number of local people who feel similarly, and who ask for rooms with fans. However, these are increasingly hard to find. Further along the coast from Kuantan there are several pleasant and unpretentious motels. I enjoyed the relaxed atmosphere of Twin Island's attractive little layout. It gets its name from the islands which are a pleasant swim from the magnificent, silent and completely deserted beach. Jane and I swam towards the islands and the sea caressed in its warmth. Then, there was a slight sting all over us, nothing painful, but sufficient to make one aware of it. It passed immediately but nothing could be seen in the clear water, and I came to the conclusion that we must have swum through a shoal of newlyborn jellyfish. It was time for tea, in any case, so we came back to the beach, where the miniature hermit crabs dig hastily into the sand as one approaches. We dried off in the heat and sat on the verandah to enjoy our tea and scones. That is one of the really nice things about Malaysia. One feels at home because all the little familiarities so dear to British hearts are there, yet the atmosphere remains exclusively that of the country. It is a splendid combination, and it will be kept, because the people themselves enjoy the superimposed extras as much as their visitors. It is amusing that it is always one's host, or one's Malaysian friends who say ... 'Oh I'm dying for my tea' ... and mean tea with all the trimmings!

Chendor Motel is similarly placed to Twin Island in that it is on the beach, but it is a much bigger place obviously used to the arrival of large parties. No doubt the Turtle season brings them, for their beach is one of the celebrated ones where the leathery turtles come between May and September to lay their eggs in the deep soft sand. So much has been written, spoken and filmed about these momentous happenings that I feel I can add little to the expert comment. There is no doubt at all that to be privileged to be present when those great, harmless creatures struggle ashore is to witness one of the great emotional moments in Nature. The turtle is so elegant in the water, turning gracefully and smoothly, yet her sortie to the steep beaches is fraught with difficulty, as she lumbers slowly, painfully, to the areas she considers 'safe'.

'SAFE!' ... the eggs are considered a great delicacy, fetching high prices and they have a quality in that they never become hard when boiled. The hard boiled quality belongs to those who rob and harass the poor creature, even sitting on her back as she gives birth to her hard-fought-for eggs. Malaysia's Government has recognised the need for conservation of the turtles, not only of the Leatherbacks on the East Coast, but of the Hawksbills who come to their Western shores. On both coasts, there are Government Hatcheries in which the eggs can be reared in safety, but this covers only a small proportion of the numbers laid, and most fall prey to predators, either greedy humans or the natural ones. But perhaps there is hope that this shameful pillage – for it is just that at the present time – can be lessened sufficiently to keep the turtles in healthy numbers. Many people realise that if the turtles should be lost, they would lose not only one of the great events in Nature's Calendar, but also a tourist attraction which is invaluable in bringing much needed foreign currency. Indeed, it may well be the turtles who provided the original incentive for the building of a large Club Méditerranée at Cherating, between Chendor and Telok Chempedak, due to be completed in 1977. I'm not sure that the East Coast is ready for the influx of such large numbers of visitors, for the developments will contain three hundred or so rooms, but there is no doubt that such development will ensure that the precious commodities of the coast must be held on to at all costs. This could be one of the rare occasions when tourism can actually help the conservationists, of which there are a growing number in Malaysia. Let us hope so, for the sake of those pathetic, vulnerable, fussy little ladies of the sea whose annual pilgrimage from the China Sea is such an unforgettable and emotional experience.

The village of Cherating is close by the designated site for the Club Méditérranee, but mercifully at the present time, it remains untouched by the coming of the new neighbours. I was invited, along with Saudi and Jane, to a 'Wayang Kulit' there, and we arrived a little early, just as the last daylight was disappearing and a sickle moon hung perilously above the palm-trees. Not a soul was to be seen, but a look at our watches told us that this was still the hour when all good Moslems were at prayer. We waited quietly in the fast gathering night, and soon, figures emerged from the lighted verandah carrying hurricane lamps and other impedimenta, towards an isloated hut. This was the Theatre, but it was explained that while it was being made ready, the villagers would like to show me some of the village activities. There is nothing more delightful than the natural courtesy of country Malay people and despite the barriers of language we got on beautifully. My poor knowledge of their language couldn't cope with the nuances and expression of dialect, but with Jane's help, and a lot of handwaving and laughing, everything was explained. I didn't need a tongue to understand the ageold duties of a kampong woman, – after all, housewives are the same in varying degrees all over the world – but I never did grasp the rules for playing chongkak! This is a game which is played in every village in some form, and consists of a piece of wood, hollowed out into sockets. The players use marbles, seeds or small stones. Everyone playing has a 'house' – one of the sockets – and the stones have to be put in the sockets in seemingly endless progressions. There must always be stones put into one's own house but not into empty ones. By the end of the game every hole must be cleared of stones. The speed with which the older ladies scooped the winnings seemed to indicate long practice and a certain amount of sleight of hand. It reminded me of Christmas games of Ludo and snakes and ladders when we all cheated like mad! Couldn't one cheat easily at this? I asked. 'Oh yes,' came the answer. 'There must be someone watching all the time.' Chongkak, or congkak must remain a puzzle. Possibly one must be born in the Kampong to unravel it.

I was shown how to prepare padi. Padi is the name of rice while it is still clad in its hard husk, and this must be removed before the grain becomes rice. A large mortar was placed on the ground, padi poured into it, and a huge, heavy pestle produced by one of the women. It was taller and heavier than she was and she proceeded to thump the padi with it. I expected the grain to fly out of the mortar but it didn't. Another woman arrived with a similar pestle and a rhythmic routine began with alternate blows at the recalcitrant padi. They stopped, poured the padi into a large flat woven tray and gently blew the dry powdery husks away, at the same time skilfully swaying and shaking the tray until magically, the husked and unhusked grains separated into two clear heaps. 'It helps, I was told, if there is a wind, then we are quicker.' In my eyes they were quick enough, and when two more and then another two women, joined the husking, pounding in quick succession so that the blows gave an even, lively rhythm, the processes were completed in no time. When ground rice is required, the pounding continues after the husks are gone. It was a clear case of many hands making light work and a fine example of the way that essential work in a community is better carried out in concert. The husking is a daily task all over South East Asia. 'How much rice is required for each person daily,' I asked. 'Each person has two rice meals. One condensed milk tin is enough for that.' Condensed milk tin! Another instance of the integration of Western habits into everyday Eastern life.

Although the women sit together, while they work at weaving, it is not community work in the strictest sense. Each piece woven is a work of art and it is here on the East Coast that the best examples are found. Peninsular Malaysia has a great variety of wild and cultivated Pandanus. One of these plants is a thorny type of cactus with orange and red fruits. This is known as Mengkuang and is used for weaving floor mats and coarser items like sacks etc. This is found inland. Other types of Pandanus are called pandan grass. One of these is used for cooking and has a special flavour that cannot be described, only tasted and sensed. Pandan cake is highly popular in Malaysia. Another grass is found near the sea, and one of these, called pandan minyak found on the East Coast, mostly in Trengganu, is smooth, thornless and excellent for dyeing into the beautiful shades found in many articles. The pandan leaves are cut as close to the main stem as possible, then split into narrow strips with the aid of a tool called jangka. The strips are then pulled repeatedly across a smooth piece of bamboo, soaked to remove resin for two days and finally dried and placed in the sun to bleach. Some of the pandan is used in this bleached state, forming the lovely wheaten colouring. The rest is dyed to red, blue, green and yellow. Formerly only natural dyes were used which restricted colouring a little and now although synthetic dyes are largely used, weavers still use these traditional colours.

The plaiting is done diagonally and starts at what eventually becomes the centre of the article. On the mat, at which one lady was working there was the most exquisite design in the finest grass weaving I have ever seen. 'Is it a traditional pattern?' I asked. She shook her head. 'No. My son designs for me, sometimes flowers, sometime like this. But most are traditional.' I looked at the mat with longing. How could I possibly carry it with me? I explained that I had 'too much barang' (luggage) and contented myself with some very pretty table mats which my suitcase could accommodate without difficulty 'Next time', I promised. 'Next time' . . . I hope so, indeed. . . .

By now there was quite a hullabaloo coming from the small hut-cum-theatre, where the front of the hut had been removed and a screen placed in its stead. Within the hut, the players were taking position. At least, that isn't quite accurate. There was an eightman orchestra with an oboe, drums, cymbals and various gongs, all going full blast, and in front of them, with a kerosene lamp between him and the screen, one man. None of this was visible to the waiting audience, composed now mainly of small squabbling boys. A chair had been placed among these for me as the guest of honour, and I accepted as gracefully as I was able. I hardly dared to admit that I would have much preferred to sit on the pandan matting with my lady friends as I had been doing while learning about the weaving. But I knew that I was expected to get up and go to see the back of the show if I wished, so I moved slightly to one side to be able to do this easily. The oboe wailed again, the cymbals increased in volume and the drums joined forces. The play began. . . .

The stories of the Wayang Kulit, the shadow plays of South East Asia, are mostly taken from the Ramayana, the Hindu epic, and by this we can see the long reaching effect that the Hindu religions and peoples have had in this part of the world for centuries. For most of that time the Wayang Kulit has been one of the main forms of cultural activity, performed on all important occasions such as weddings, births, circumcisions, and on occasion invoking the spirits to look kindly on harvests or fishing fleets. Prior to the advent of electricity and the kerosene lamp, the shadows were formed by the use of a cotton wick. Shadows of what? There are all sorts of characters. Gods and kings, hero and heroine, funny man and ogre, all of them puppets. The outlines are all traditional and traced on paper, then pasted on buffalo hide which has been scraped smooth, cut out with a sharp knife and stiffened with manoeuvrable bamboo slivers. I once watched an artist from Cheng Mai in Northern Thailand doing this work, and it demands a very great degree of artistry and delicacy. The figures are painted in brilliant hues. These colours are not seen by the watchers of the screen, but they help the puppetteer to distinguish between the 'players' in his half dark dream world. For instance, the Maharaja Rawana, the Ogre King, always has a black face and pointed nails. Hanuman, the whitefaced Monkey God, always has a tail and a tongue. Siti Dewi, the heroine, is always petite and pretty and her stalwart prince has a spear to show his gallantry and is always dark green. There are palace outlines, comic interludes, all the ingredients of pantomime, tragedy and high drama, and all of it is performed by one man, the Tok Dalang, or Spinner of Stories, as he selects his characters and waves them delicately towards the screen on banana stems, changing his voice to suit the story's development. One very interesting thing for the lovers of theatrical history: the goodies are kept on his right and the baddies are always on his left. . . . The story wound through the adventures of Sri Rama in his efforts to rescue his beloved from the clutches of the Ogre King, absorbing the audience which had been reinforced now by the weavers and padi huskers, and various other individuals who just materialised out of nowhere. I quietly moved to peep behind the scenes. I'm not sure which was more entrancing . . . the faces of the grown-ups and kids out front, or the scene which now came before me. The Tok Dalang, accompanied by his faithful orchestra were all engaged in the gentle unhurried movements which make Malays so graceful in every activity, but among them sat a small child. She was motionless, no more than three years old, sitting between the protective legs of one of the musicians, but starlight was in her eyes as she watched the magic of the fairytale so close to her tiny hands. It was probably the first time she had seen the Tok Dalang and his dream-making. And, for one precious moment I was her age, and watching Peter Pan for the very first time. . . .

The Wayang Kulit was still going when we left nearly two hours later and showed no signs of flagging. I'm told that it goes on as long as the audience stays. By the look of them, they were far from weary of the Tok Dalang and his prodigious memory, and I was glad. While he stays in favour surely the spirits of the East Coast will stay to protect the unsophisticated, charming people who live there, and the grave of the mermaid, said to have been washed ashore some ninety years ago, will always be tended as it is today.

'I think you should visit the Panching Caves,' said Saudi next morning. 'Put jeans on, and good shoes, for you'll have to climb a bit.' 'Like the Batu Caves,' I said brightly remembering our sortie there together. 'Higher,' he said briefly, 'and there isn't a railway.'

I groaned mentally but cheered myself by thinking of the weight I must inevitably lose. We drove some way northeastwards out of Kuantan towards Sungei Lembing, where the deep mine is, and then along an old track through a rubber plantation. Ahead, rising out of the flat plain, was a great limestone cliff, and we stopped at its foot. A little Malay came to meet us, and as I steppped out of the car, I felt like royalty with the great military salute he gave me, along with a beamingly toothless smile. We walked past a small hut where the chickens squawked away from our feet, and started upwards.

The steps were steep and wide apart, sometimes cuts in the rock and sometimes an iron ladder, and the handrail consisted of a rusty iron pipe and then a piece of rope. It was a tiring climb, and, by the time we reached the top, sweat ran from my hair over the length of my body into my shoes so that I felt that I'd stepped from the sauna. We paused a moment to get our breath, and admire the tremendous view, then started downwards around several large rocks and into a cave. This is a very different place to Batu Caves, and is the home of a different religion. It was discovered some years ago by a Thai Buddhist monk, who asked the Sultan for permission to turn it into a shrine. He laboured for years, carrying most of the materials by himself, and still lives in its close vicinity. Once through the narrow entrance and used to the gloom, one finds oneself in a huge cavern, lit only by narrow slits hundreds of feet above and through which the blessed daylight filters. Silence reigns, except for the squeaking of the disturbed bats, and somewhere in the darkness, the constant dripping of water. Our guide paused to switch on lights which illuminated a passage far ahead, and we followed him across the echoing cave, and round a jagged corner to find an altar, surrounded with name tablets, but this wasn't our goal. Across another great cavern in the half light, supplied by a intermittent string of light bulbs, and then suddenly a blaze of illumination, and I found myself looking at a large gilt statue of the Sleeping Buddha, measuring all of 30 feet. In front of the statue, on a small table, were a number of small boxes with the familiar fortune-telling sticks. The idea is to shake a box gently, and patiently, thinking of the required prayer, until just one bamboo stick falls out, alone, on the table. Then, one looks at the number, and takes it to a nearby notice-board, where hang strings of coloured tickets of the type received in cloakrooms and raffles. One chooses the number found on the fortune stick, puts a contribution in the box, and reads the fortune on the reverse side of the ticket. Mine wasn't too bad, so I decided to believe it. My companions weren't too pleased with theirs so had another shot at getting better ones. All this time, the Buddha slept with that gentle, implacable smile on his gilded face, and I thought we were alone with him. But my Malay guide led me to the far side of the cave, and there, in the darkness, I saw that a large tortoise lay in some dampish mud. It raised its head as we approached and the guide brought him a plate with food on it.

'I feed him every day,' he said.

'How did he get here?'

'Someone brought him as a gift for Buddha.'

'How long has he been here.'

'Oh, long time now, memo.'

A wave of distress swept over me. Surely, the Great Lord Buddha, with all his tremendous compassion, wouldn't have wished this helpless creature to be condemned to live its long life in the darkness of a dank cave?

The Malay saw how I felt, and in his understanding, nodded. 'I don't like him being here either, so I come to see him often. Two weeks ago I had operation in hospital, but now come again.'

I moved away across the cavern, away from the sleeping statue, over the rough floor of the first cave to the daylight at the opening, but the sense of oppression stayed with me, even while we clambered over rocks further up the cliff face to a Chinese altar in yet another cave two hundred feet above, and then slipped and slid downward again, down the rusty iron steps. Even now, I find myself thinking often of the Prisoner of Panching Caves, and wish that I had had the courage to bring him away from that loneliness and darkness. My only consolation is that a small wiry, compassionate little man climbs every day to see him. May he be spared for a long time to do that, for even a tortoise likes company

Kuala Trengganu still shows some of its British influences: large bungalows which are the outward relics of Colonial administrations, a big traffic roundabout on the outskirts and a golf course. South-East Asians share Britain's mania for sport. Football, badminton, horseracing and golf all flourish like the proverbial green bay tree, and the last named has a special place in Kuala Trengganu because the Municipal course there claims to be the oldest in Malaysia. It was built in the 1920s when the Sultan caught the golf craze from an English administrator. Look for it near the beach on the outskirts of the town. Look also for a small building across the road from the Sultan's modern palace. It is now a small museum and showplace, but once it formed part of the private apartments belonging to the Sultan's family. It was torn down from its original site and rebuilt in its present position.

I wasn't greatly impressed with Kuala Trengganu at first, but perhaps I'm being unfair. I arrived, hot, tired, longing for a swim in the clear blue rippling sea, and already a little put out by the news that there was no point in going back to Rantau Abang because the locals said that the turtles had not yet put in an appearance that season. I had wanted to see if the new restrictions on the treatment of the turtles were helping to prevent their molestation. But the opportunity was apparently not to be forthcoming. Instead we made our way to D.O.T's Motel, which is perched atop a small bukit (hill) near the broadcasting station, with a delightful view all the way to the sea. It is some way from that sea and from the town. The Motel is a pleasant attractive little place, but it was spoiled by the unusable condition of its swimming pool. They had started working on it, so other travellers will hopefully be more fortunate than I. Trengganu was also the one place in all Malaysia, indeed in the whole of South-East Asia, where I was badly bitten by sandflies. Normally, I am immune from bites of this kind, but there seemd to be nothing normal about the sandfly population of Trengganu. So be warned and go prepared. There were no ill-effects, apart from a face which looked like 'spotted dog'. Malaria is well controlled although there are occasional outbreaks of dengue. One doesn't die from dengue, only wishes to! This all sounds a little unkind to a nice little town which provided me with several unique experiences. It isn't meant to be. I particularly liked the colourful market which takes place in the courtyard of a modern concrete building. The fruits, vegetables, food stalls, etc., are heaped in confusion with the vendors sitting cheek by jowl exchanging gossip and jokes. As always, the fish market, within the cool concrete ground floor, provided tantalising glimpses of the sea's riches, many unknown to Western eyes, and the first floor surrounding the courtyard is given over to silk and batik merchants, mostly Indians, whose wares are heaped in brilliant profusion. It doesn't pay to accept the first price asked. We had, as a matter of fact, bought at much better prices the evening before in Jalan Kampong China, before going for a super curry at one of the night stalls. Later I kicked myself for not attempting to carry two of everything, particularly the pretty bajus (short blouse or jacket), for bargaining had produced a very fair price. Another time, I went to see the brassware which has become a popular souvenir of East Coast Malaysia. I was told I was going to a factory. This turned out to be two primitive sheds beside small attap village houses and any self-respecting factory inspector in Britain would have turned grey on the spot, for the workers toiled in semi-darkness to turn out the beautiful pieces. Granted, one must always remember that darkness brings some measure of relief from the tropical heat, but there were unguarded furnace heat fires, dangerous for the unwary. The process is simple enough. The mould is first designed according to the shape of the item required and wax poured in for the impression. The case is removed and sprayed with layers of clay. This is then baked and dried until red-hot, and molten brass poured into it. When the metal hardens, the clay is removed and the piece is ready for the engravers. Conditions were little better for the batik workers, and I was happier when I visited cottage industries in other places who dealt only with batik, but one must remember that all these people work for themselves, their families joining in the work, so who am I to change habits of a lifetime. The nicest experience came when I was invited into the little house of one family nearby, for, sitting on the rush matting of the cool interior, was a brandnew Mum, with her two-day old baby son. I'd never seen such a little Malay before, and he was very sweet. What was interesting too, was the array, all around her on the rush matting, of all the modern impedimenta of the newly born. Again, this transition into today from the traditions of yesterday and the day before.

Kota Bahru, the northernmost town of importance on the East Coast, also has an excellent morning market, but most of the activity takes place on the pavements, so that products spill over on to the roads and are inextricably mixed with parking signs, tri-shaws and motorbikes. Hapless chickens, panting in the heat next to mounds of shining green watermelons, slippery silver fish alongside a rainbowed heap of cheap cottons, and all sold with great panache by cheerful souls with the greatest variety of hats anywhere in Malaysia. These head-dresses are part of the fascination. They consist of bright materials swathed over straw hats or simply twisted around a woman's head to leave artistic angles in the folded cloth, but they fulfil their object, which is to keep the wearer's head protected from the full rays of the sun. But around the corner, in the shade, I found women with different hats. These were two young Malay girls in the smart gray uniform of the Malay Police. Their neat caps at the correct angle, they looked the very epitome of New Malaysia and a world away from the market.

In Kota Bahru, known to all as K.B., I caught up with a Wild West Show. Imagine going all the way East to find Buffalo Bill, Red Indians, covered waggons and the like. I'd seen their posters at various intervals, advertising their coming or their going, but it wasn't until I stayed at Hotel Kesina that they were 'in the flesh'. It was the hair that attracted my attention for the be-jeaned Americans were wearing theirs very long indeed, for their parts in the show. Malaysian hairstyles have become longer than the short back and sides of former time, but even so, the heat precludes the very long styles for most men. I watched the showpeople with some interest for they were putting some effort into the promotion of their presentation with a teepee, set up in the hotel lobby, it looked a bit strange with Malay and Chinese girls selling the tickets. Kesina is average; its restaurant likewise, but adequate. As usual, I preferred the shophouse cafes where one perches on small stools at marble topped tables. Hardly conducive to a long sojourn over dinner, but the food is good and cheap and the atmosphere is a far cry from our own Western environment. It is these sights and sounds which are so inviting in the early evening. Curries, the slightly acrid smell of fried mee, the rosy prawns, each as large as a Scandinavian crayfish, a pile of sliced pineapple, the small helpings of rice folded into leaves and tied with the stem. My tongue waters at the thought.

My sandfly bites were irritating, so I went in search of a remedy in the 'jenny all things' shop next door to Hotel Kesina. Chinese grocers sell everything from postcards and stamps to tinned fruitcake, from dried fish to frozen food, and from kaolin poultices to Coca-Cola, so insect bite ointment was not beyond the bounds of possibility. The shopkeeper suggested Tiger Balm. 'Now kind,' he said. 'This is white now, not brown.' It said in the pamphlet that the cream would act as insect repellent. I wasn't surprised when I used it. Hardly conducive to attracting anything, or anybody. But I dabbed it on and hoped for the best. It works, for by morning the angry lumps had paled, so from now on, my advice to all would-be visitors to Malaysia is that no trip is complete without Tiger Balm's latest cure-all!

No visit to Kota Bahru would be complete without a visit to the Beach of Passionate Love, so Saudi, Jane and I set off to go there. The name dates from the Second World War. Before that time the beach was called Semut Api, which means fire ant. There are a lot of these little creatures in Malaysia and probably they live on the beach too. Most people find them by sitting on lallang grass or a treestump and getting bitten, but they are quite harmless and the stinging bite passes immediately. The origin of the new name is uncertain, but it is believed that it was coined by Commandos during the Japanese occupation. In any event it was immortalised by Gerry Gaskin in his book of that name. Mr. Gaskin and I once belonged to the same Dramatic Society. I always hoped I might appear as a character in one of his books, but alas for aspirations! His book contained some brilliantly accurate descriptions of East Coast life, and though some of the festivals no longer happen in quite the same way, I would recommend it to anyone interested in reading more about the area. In any event the beach is wide, beautiful, and usually deserted during the week. Not quite deserted on this occasion, because several of the Wild West troupe were disporting themselves in the warm waves, and a graceful Malay woman, clad in baju kurung and sarong carried a large basket of driftwood on her head, adding small pieces as she walked slowly along. There is a hotel with twelve rooms and a small bar beside the beach, and, I quote from information received 't.v. on request'. I can't imagine anyone wanting the facile glamour of the box when outside, is the velvet softness of a tropical night on one of the loveliest beaches anywhere. Yet occasionally, such beauty is unbearably poignant, so perhaps the diversion could be welcome.

The road from the beach traverses little wooden bridges across bubbling streams, beside which rows of gaily coloured washing hang, belonging presumably to the nearby kampong. Only, on closer inspection, it isn't washing at all, but lines of newly printed batik, hung in the sun to dry, and the boys in the brown stream aren't just playing, they are washing away the final traces of extraneous dye, from the cloth. All the little houses handmake batik in this area and produce the best in Malaysia. One wanders freely from house to house inspecting the stock and removing one's shoes at each shop, for in each case the wares are shown in private houses and the materials share the room with the everyday requirements of living. Patterns can be modern, or stylised as most of the Indonesian batek (batik is the same word) is, and are created by stamping wax design on the white cotton. The cloth is then dipped into dye of the required colour and stamped and re-dyed until the patterns are produced. On some, colours are handpainted into the cloth into spaces left by the wax and in this freehand styling there are always differences in the patterns. All of them are truly beautiful, immensely varied and very reasonably priced. Every possible use is made of batik. Tablecloths, bedspreads, handbags with matching hats, shirts, etc., and of course in the traditional sarong lengths. Jane wanted one of these, and as usual in any transaction in Malaysia there was a certain amount of haggling over the cost. Try as she might, she couldn't get it below a certain figure which I considered reasonable in any case. (Saudi had long given up and retired to read his newspaper in the shade of a banana tree) 'Take it,' said I. 'You'll be sorry if you don't and batik is more expensive in K.L.' That did it. 'O.K.' she said. 'I'll take it, but' . . . as a final winning shot, 'give me extra!' Many of these villagers specialise in kain songket, that exquisite material, interwoven with silver and gold thread, used in the national dress worn by men on formal occasions. It is expensive, but not in comparison to Western cloths and if you have money to spare, and are going to the East Coast, wait until you get to Trengganu or K.B. to buy it. You'll have the time of your life. I don't know when I enjoyed an afternoon's shopping more, than that occasion, on the way back from the Beach of Passionate Love. It was completed when I met a baboon riding a bike . . . well, his master was riding and he was perched on the handlebars and obligingly posed for a picture.

Another good buy in Kelantan is silver, for some of the most beautiful pieces are handmade in K.B. You can see the work by visiting Kampong Sireh. The men work in a dull little room, each at a small school desk, engaged in the most delicate and intricate tasks. One may be putting the finishing touches to a character from the Mamayana for a place marker to grace a formal dinner table. Another is polishing a newly completed rosebowl. Yet another is hammering fine filigree into a delicate flower motif. Kelantan silver is justly famous for its beauty and many of the patterns have been used for 600 years by families who have handed on the art. Nowadays, machines are used to spin the silver thread, but until recently all work from the ingot stage to the final presentation was done by hand. All the hammering, shaping, etc., is still done that way. I can testify too, to its durability, for I have used Kelantan silver daily for over twenty years, though of course, one is very careful. It has increased greatly in cost with the general rise in world prices for silver, but I'm not sure that the artist who fashions it is any better off than his grandfather was. Perhaps his main repayment is in his own creation of beauty at his little desk.

It would be very pleasant if one could drive across Malaysia to Perak, Kedah and Penang. But this is not possible at the present time. Plans are in hand to finish the central section of the road, through the jungle, but there has been considerable harassment of workers by terrorists, working under Communist directives, and until the hazard is removed by Malaysian troops, one goes by air. It is a pity. But Malaysian Airline's domestic routes are very efficient, and one gets an excellent view all the way to Penang, so there are many compensations. Still, one leaves the East Coast with great regret. It can only be a matter of time before it catches up with the rest of Malaysia but, in the meantime, it is extremely precious for its glimpse of the pace at which yesterday moved. An unhurried, peaceful pace to which, from the distance of frenetic London, one looks back and longs to return.

6. Pearls in the North

Within a few yards of the steps of the Merlin Hotel in Georgetown on the island of Penang, a frangipani tree grows, its white flowers dropping their fragrant petals over the wall which separates it from the incessant traffic on a oneway carousel. They fall also upon a grave. Seldom visited now, but, standing beside it recently I wondered what the man whose mortal remains rest there would make of the modern trappings of tourism that Penang wears. Francis Light, sea captain, and possible entrepreneur, would undoubtedly approve of much that has been done to make 'his' island into Malaysia's leading tourist resort. In spite of all that the purists might say, Penang has not so far, been guilty of many of the mistakes that have been made elsewhere in the East, and though this may be more by luck than anything else, Light would have understood that too. Luck is often the two-headed fairy that guides man's destinies, and Luck had its part in Light's life along with commonsense and an inestimable patience. It was in 1771 that Francis Light first espied the lovely island called Pulau Ka Satu. Single island in the old legends, and considered that it would make an excellent harbour for victualling, watering and repairing ships of the Honourable East India Company. This was despite the island's reputation as a haven for the Lanuns, the pirates who had been the terror of coastal shipping for generations, making the Spice Run one of the most risky in the Far East. Light reported his find to Warren Hastings, but it wasn't until 1786 that he received permission to negotiate with the Sultan of Kedah for the island. At this time the island was known as

Pulau Pinang (Betel Nut Island) but when Light successfully completed his bargaining with the Sultan and finally hoisted his flag at the spot now covered by Fort Cornwallis, he renamed it, as he said in his proclamation, to be . . . 'now named the Prince of Wales Island . . . this eleventh day of August, one thousand seven hundred and eightysix, being the eve of the Prince of Wales Birthday.' To enable the land near the harbour to be cleared by his band of somewhat reluctant Indians for this historic moment, Light undertook what must be regarded as one of the most original schemes ever. He loaded his cannon with silver dollars and fired it into the jungle. The land was cleared and the first camp established almost as quickly as it has taken to write this. . . .

Light declared the island a free port, to encourage merchants and traders to come to the new settlement, and within six years no less than ten thousand had made their way there, mostly Chinese and Malays. Indians came too, firstly as sepoys with the British, but then, as in Singapore, becoming police and merchants. In the year 1800, the strip of land on the mainland opposite to Penang was also ceded to the English by the Sultan, and named Province Wellesley. Penang flourished, and it was partially due to its rapid advancement that Malacca gradually declined. Light died in 1804, so he never lived to see Penang become a presidency in 1805 and given equal status with Bengal and Bombay. Nor could he know that in that same year Nelson was to win the Battle of Trafalgar and that the plans for a base and naval dockyard at Penang were abandoned. It is a pity too for the history books, that Light didn't live to see Stamford Raffles visit Penang for the first time. He came in the entourage of a new Governor, but his stars didn't designate him for Penang. He was to go Southwards. . . .

I think that Penang owes much to that fact, for just as it was the establishment of Penang which removed the necessity for Malacca, so Penang too developed at a much slower rate after Singapore's founding, remaining mercifully rural with only Georgetown, its little capital, having any leanings towards the trappings of the modern world. This was also in part due to the realisation that Penang's topography, with its hilly heart, made for a healthy place in which to live, though the real problem was how to get up and down the hills. Someone suggested a railway. It was tried, but didn't work, and it wasn't until 1923 that the present system was evolved. The rest of the island stayed in its natural state apart from a new nutmeg plantation, until rubber came into the picture. Fishing remained the main source of income for most of the country people, while Georgetown retained its merchants and immigrants. It is because of this evolvement that Georgetown and its immediate environs hold most of the things of interest for tourists, and it is in this area that the hotels have sprung up, catering for the rapidly increasing number of people who find their way on package tours to the newer playgrounds of the Far East. Many of the hotels are situated along Batu Ferringhi. Translated, that is Beach of the Foreigners, due to the presence during Colonial times of one or two small hotels which catered for Europeans on what was known as local leave. It is a delightful location for today's holidaymakers, staying in Merlin Beach Club, Rasa Sayang, Lone Pine and many more and it is easy to get a taxi or bus into Georgetown for shopping or sightseeing, and in addition most of the tour operators and travel agents run excursions from these hotels, as well as from the ones in Georgetown.

It is a long time since I first visited the E and O Hotel. I came there one bright morning directly from my long three week voyage from England. It was in those days all that I expected to find in a hotel of the type immortalised by Somerset Maugham in his depiction of colonial living, and it was my first introduction to a way of life which I knew was not going to last. Yet, going back into the E and O after an absence of many years, I found it had changed very little, apart from the trimmings added by a new wing and other 1976 essentials, and the presence of far more international clientele. It still has the same high ceilinged, spacious rooms, impeccable service and excellent food in the tradition started when the Sarkies constructed (the E & O was hardly 'built') the place in 1884. They have an excellent Austrian chef, and a China born chef who doesn't look a day over 40, though he is nearly 60. Maybe it's due to the magnificence of the food he cooks. He doesn't speak a word of English or Malay, even after 40 years in Penang so it was quite a pantomime to get a recipe out of him. To add to the problems my recorder ran out of steam so the result sounded like the Chipmunks ... in Chinese. Still I managed to get the main ingredients of one dish, so until you can try it at the E & O, try it from the receipts at the end of the book. I must admit that the bills, if staying at the E & O hardly fit into economy class. But how else can one pay for nostalgia, on a grand scale.

The Merlin across the road, is not cheap either. None of the top class hotels are. But they are universally good. Even in the cheaper grades, standards are high. However I must admit I am biased, and make no apology for it. Let me show you some of the reasons why I find Penang, tourist warts and all, such an attractive place in which to spend days on the edge of the Malaysian world.

Within walking distance of the E & O and Merlin are some historically interesting places. Fort Cornwallis, a playground and garden by day is an open air eating house by night. There's little left of the original fort but on one of the ramparts you'll find the Penang Cannon. It was presented to the Sultan of Johore in 1606 by the Dutch. Seven years later it was taken under seige to Java, where it remained for 100 years or so, and was then thrown into the Malacca Straits by pirates. In 1880 it was salvaged, cleaned up and brought to its present resting place. Local women believe that if they place flowers in the barrel of Seri Rambai, they will be rewarded by the gift of children.

Right next to the old fort, you'll see a clock tower. You can't miss it really because all the traffic merry-go-rounds about it. The clock was a presentation to the city by a Mr. Cheah Chin Gok to commemorate Queen Victoria's Diamond Jubilee. A few steps away, past the Government buildings with their imposingly shaded porticos, is the Penang Museum. This claims to have the best collection of Chinese carved furniture in Malaysia, including a Chinese bridal chamber. More interesting to anyone looking for peculiarly 'Penang' things, is the handwritten will of Francis Light, together with many sketches which show Penang in its very early days, and the collections of local tools, birds, beasts and butterflies and krisses. Unique even in South -East Asia, is the collection of awards given to Tunku Abdul Rahman while he was Premier of the new nation of Malaysia. One would have expected this to be in Kuala Lumpur, but Penang has a prior claim for another special reason. The British had set up the first school in Penang in 1821 in this very building, and it was here that the Tunku, a member of the Royal House of Kedah who owned Penang until it was ceded to the British, was sent to school. When the Tunku heard that his old schoolhouse was going to be pulled down in the 1960s he personally requested that it should be spared, and it was turned into a museum, and enhanced with his personal collection in due course. I wonder how many schoolboys would have a like affection for their place of torment?

Also in Farquhar Street is the Church of St. George the Martyr, the first church built for Anglican worship in Malaysia and now an historical monument, though continuing its services. Designed by Captain R. Smith who was responsible for many of the fine sketches in the Penang Museum, the church was built by the effort of convict labour, brought from Indian Penal Settlements. If you look on the corner steps you'll find the sign which marked their work. The present building was restored after the Second World War, and there are many Chinese, Malays, and Indians among the regular congregation, though of course by far the majority of the Penang population still retain their old beliefs.

The places in which to worship in these religions are among the most interesting and they are legion. My own favourite is that of Kuan Yin, Buddhist Goddess of Mercy in Pitt Street. It isn't impressive, it isn't large, but it lives. People bring their troubles to the gentle goddess, who listens to all pleadings. She is a Bodhisattva, that is, one who rejected entry into Nirvana as long as there is pain and injustice on earth. In the courtyard outside, you will see large pot bellied stoves belching forth smoke, as jossmoney burns constantly inside. The joss-sticks and candles are taken inside the temple where the atmosphere is just as thick, and fruit, cakes, cooked chickens, etc, are piled on the altars, their wrappers lying discarded on the floors as kneeling figures shake the fortune sticks to receive answers to their problems from the divinity who stretches out her arms towards them.

You'll have to take a taxi to reach another Buddhist temple of a very different kind. This is Kek Lok Si, built on a hillside above Ayer Itam, and inspired by a vision given to a Buddhist priest in 1885. Certainly the result is dreamlike. The Million Buddahs Precious Pagoda floats high above one in the clear blue air, but it is reached through a warren of souvenir shops, wedged on the shallow steadily climbing stairs in highly realistic fashion. You can buy anything here, but you'll have to bargain very hard indeed to beat the shopkeepers whose long ears hear the price you are offered on the next stall and immediately cut it, so one is never sure if it is a real bargain or not, unless primed beforehand with an accurate assessment of worth. Finally you'll arrive at the pagodas, the myriad altars and the fish ponds, whose tortoise inmates are as old as the building. Don't attempt Kek Lok Si unless you are sound in wind and limb, for it is very tiring on a hot day. But, if you *can* manage it, the effort is well worth while. There is still a monastery there, but sadly the numbers are dwindling and now there are only nine men to keep the huge place in order. No-one comes to replace them, so what happens when they go? Probably Lord God Buddha has made provision for that.

Back in Anson Road in Georgetown there is another Buddhist temple, completely devoid of the joss-sticks, money stoves, and hawkers which characterise the other two. This is the Penang Buddhist Association Temple and is obviously a place which has been well endowed. The Statues are pure white marble, and represent Lord Buddha and his disciples. Magnificent paintings show the story of his Life, illuminated by superb crystal chandeliers especially imported from Czechoslovakia. There is serenity here. Wat Chayamangkalaram Temple is quiet too, for it is for meditation of a different kind. This is the Thai Temple in Burmah Lane, and the main area is taken up with a 108 foot statue of the Reclining Buddha surrounded by serpents and giants, whose job it is to keep watch from the other world. The walls are lined from floor to ceiling with little golden plaques each bearing a name. It was only when walking round the back of the great golden statue that I happened to peep into a small door and found where the ashes of the dear departed were placed. They are all in niches, in nice tidy rows under the great figure, so this temple is an extension of the crematorium. Before leaving I put some money into a prayer wheel and spun for my fortune. It wasn't nearly as satisfactory as others foretold in Hong Kong and in Panching so I chose not to believe it. But in retrospect, it has been far more accurate!

Not tired of temples yet? Splendid, because there are several more which are musts. Still in Georgetown is the Khoo Kongsi in Cannon Square, reached by the 'secret' Leong San Tong alley. This is just off Pitt Street, so you could go there after visiting Kuan Yin, but you'll have to ask your way. Kongsi have been part of the traditions of old China for hundreds of years when people with the same surnames built meeting halls in order to keep together in clans or tongs. The habit came to Penang with its Chinese immigrants and the original Khoos came to the island in junks about the beginning of the nineteenth century, and in 1850 bought the land in Cannon Square converting a large house into a temple. It was designed in the manner of a palace of old China and was so impressive that many of the clan were afraid that they might offend the Emperor by being too pretentious. The very night after the building was completed the roof was burned off, so, when it was rebuilt, it was on a lesser scale. Nevertheless it is very picturesque with gilded verandahs, curving roofs, with glazed porcelain tiles and intricate carving where dragons hold glass spheres representing fire, moon or the sun. The dragons, who alone have the power to play in the sky, bring wealth and fertility. They seem to have done rather well by the Khoos.

I was shown around by a charming Indian who is the caretaker for the Kongsi and who is a positive mine of information on the building. He showed me the central shrine, where the gods of prosperity, happiness and longevity hold court behind red lacquer and gold leaf. We walked into the ancestral shrines where wooden tablets bearing the names of deceased Khoos, and called Sinchoo, are placed around the patron saints, and on the walls are more gold plaques as seen in the Buddhist temple. These too commemorate the dead, but in this instance are reserved for those who have brought distinction to the Clan. Gendar Singh then took me to see the Dogs of Fo, standing in the courtyard. These beasts are a lion and a lioness carved in greeny granite. 'Look,' he said, 'There is a marble ball inside the lion's mouth. See if you can get it out.' I duly obeyed, but no matter how I struggled, it was impossible. Gendar Singh chuckled. 'I try every day,' he said. 'They say that if someone can remove the ball with his bare hand he will be the luckiest man on earth. The builder knew what he was doing. . . .'

The buildings around the perimeter of the square belong to the Kongsi, and immediately opposite there is a theatre where plays and operas are performed on special occasions. Gendar Singh told me that at one time there had been a suggestion from the Penang Government that the building merited a more imposing entrance and that this could be achieved if some of the old houses were demolished. But the Kongsi declined. Hence the almost secret approach through the tiny, mean streets, into this fairytale square. At the end of my tour, I proffered a tip to my invaluable guide, but he refused courteously. 'It is my pleasure,' he said. A remarkable occurrence in these mercenary days and worthy of record.

I never thought, in my wildest dreams, that I would be invited to play maternity nurse to a poisonous snake. But that is exactly what happened when I visited the most famous of all Penang's multitudinous temples, the Temple of Azure Cloud, better known as the Snake Temple. This is situated along the road from the airport, and if you arrive in Penang by air, look out for it on your way to the hotel. The temple was built in 1873 and is dedicated to a god known as Chor Soo Kong. According to the tale, he was a monk who possessed magical powers, but on examining them, he might just have been exceptionally good at sleight of hand. Nevertheless, he was highly revered and the shrine was built around ashes brought from joss-sticks burned in front of his image in China. As the money poured in to maintain his shrine the present building was erected at Sungei Kluang. Local snakes moved in as the builders moved out and have stayed in residence ever since, so contrary to belief, it is *not* the snakes which are the object of worship. They are considered to be guardians of the deity and as such are holy, and harmless. I'd hardly call them that. They are, after all, pit vipers, and although they are doped with joss, they are poisonous. The caretaker of the shrine told me that he has been bitten so many times that he only gets small reactions now but that in the beginning he had a paralysed arm for a day or two. I hoped I wouldn't be in the same state . . . snakes are everywhere, around the altars, on the lamp standards, under the shrines and around the candlesticks. They are an irridescent green and measure twelve inches or more. But in the branches of a small tree there were tiny ones like large worms. These were new born. I was taken into the 'labour room'. This was a corner of the shrine and consisted of a ladder with pads of newspapers placed below and around it. On the ladder were several large female snakes, and as I watched, one dropped a sac from her body. It splashed down on the newspaper. My companion reached down with a pair of tongs and removed a tiny struggling creature from the wet mess, washed it in a small dish and placed it among the branches of the waiting tree. No less than six were delivered this way, while I 'assisted'. I don't recommend it as an afternoon's entertainment every day, or as an occupation, but it is certainly worth seeing, at least once. There used to be a huge python long ago. On my first visit to the Temple with my small daughter, she had liked the little snakes, but taken an immediate aversion to the big one, and I hadn't blamed her. I didn't enquire where the monster had gone. Probably eaten, for python is a delicacy. . . .

There are many more places of worship in Penang, including both Muslim and Hindu temples. As I have described many of the activities closely connected with these religions in considerable detail elsewhere in these pages, I don't propose to reiterate them. But if you are going no further into Malaysia than Penang, and happen to arrive on the right days, you may see these ceremonies at the appropriate place of worship. Perhaps that is one of the comforts of religion whichever it may be. There are universal patterns. . . .

A multitude of information on every conceivable aspect of life in Penang can be obtained from their excellent Tourist Organisation. I recommend you to them. Your hotel can direct you to their offices, or information bureaux.

From Sungei Kluang, let's go onward for a short trip around the island. Beaches are lovely and remote, villages look as if they have slumbered under the coconut trees forever, and the cool greenness of the hill roads is marvellous after the sweat of sightseeing in Georgetown, or even after the sophistication of the hotels along Batu Ferringhi. You can't get lost, for the road circles the island and it runs through a paradise of tropical trees such as rambutans, papaya, mangosteens, bananas and nutmegs. They don't all fruit at once of course, so you cannot possibly taste them all unless you stay a year, but if you are lucky, you'll find small stalls along the road where you can find the local fruit in season. Buy dried chopped nutmeg, plastic packed now so it is easy to bring home as a souvenir. In mangosteen season, remember the juice stains, so don't drop it on a white dress, as I did.

At the south-eastern tip of the island not far from the airport, is Batu Muang, where the fishing boats are usually high on the beach. There is a shrine here dedicated to Admiral Cheng Ho. He is supposed to have left his footprint on a stone at this point. He must have been a bit of a giant, for its companion print is on Langkawi, sixty miles north of Penang!

Before going back to the hotel, take a train to the top of Penang Hill. We'll wait in company with a crowd of local people for the little funicular, most of whom will alight at the various stops to reach their own homes. It is very little different to catching the 8.20 a.m. to Waterloo . . . at least, it seemed to be so on the last occasion I was there, for there was an elderly Englishman complete with brief case (but sans bowler hat) who shook his Straits Times in exasperation while looking at his watch and complaining that 'things were not what they should be and that the train was consistently late'. There'll always be an England while spirits like his straddle the globe. . . .

One of my Chinese friends lived on the Hill during the Second World War, along with her family and sisters. The girls were justifiably afraid of the Japanese, who frequently went looking for candidates for their brothels, willing or not, and at the first hint of 'company', the family hid all the girls below the floorboards. My friend told me that they also had a pact between themselves, that should one of them have the misfortune to be caught then she would go quietly to save the others. This luckily never became necessary for despite occasional visits by the soldiery, the hiding place was never in danger. Now, years later, the family's main memory is of the very long walk they had up and down the hill if anything was required in Georgetown because the railway wasn't working for a while. Looking from the relative comfort of the wooden seats of the funicular's crowded cabin, I see what they mean. It is several degrees cooler at the top of the hill, and you can get a meal at the hotel if wishing to stay a little longer while admiring the breathtaking view. Take a cardigan in the evening, when the lights of Georgetown and the ships in the Straits nearly three thousand feet below make the hill among the most romantic settings in South-East Asia.

I haven't mentioned Penang's Botanical Gardens. They are particularly pretty, and immaculate in the manner of all such gardens in Malaysia, and they still have their tribes of monkeys living more or less amicably together. I was so very pleased to see them, and to see the way in which local people still care about them. I only hope that their eventual fate will be kinder than that of their brothers in Singapore's Gardens.

I also haven't mentioned one word about shopping, vital to the holiday plans of most women and to more than a few of their menfolk, despite assurances to the contrary. Penang is easily the best place in Malaysia in which to find your souvenirs and is less expensive for many things than Kuala Lumpur, and, if you aren't going to Singapore, you should do your shopping there, apart from the regional 'buys' already mentioned. Choice is varied. You'll find batek too, made in factories visited by tour buses, and though they are not the strictly handmade types found on the East Coast, they are reasonably priced and of many colours and designs. Jewellery boxes, carvings, rotan and basketwork, etc., and a wider selection of Kelantan silver than I found anywhere else, including Kelantan itself. Photographic equipment is available at good prices, although not in comparison with Singapore or Hong Kong. Remember that it is expected that you will bargain in most places. In any case do shop around. It pays. For antiques look in Rope Street, and for purely fun shopping try the Pasar Malam (night market) which as in Singapore, moves house each night.

To get to the shopping districts you can take a taxi if you've no desire to walk. They are easy to see because their tops are painted yellow. If you don't get one at the hotel, you can be almost certain that a cruising taxi will see you walking and stop. Make sure the meter works before you get in, and then all is well. Tri-shaws are fun to try if you don't object to human-power, but these are more expensive than petrol driven transport, and you would be wise to negotiate a price before you start. There is also an abundance of buses, and fares are reasonable. The city terminus is at Leboh Victoria, but private buses have their own terminals. They go to most of the tourist destinations. The Tourist Office produces a useful booklet with all service details, but if you arrive in Penang and go out to Batu Ferringhi before getting a copy, the blue bus goes into Jalan Maxwell, in the centre of Georgetown. The long distance bus to Kuala Lumpur leaves from Butterworth pier on the mainland. It leaves daily at 9 a.m., arriving in K.L. at 5.30 p.m. The fare at the time of writing is 16 Malay dollars, but no doubt it will have gone up. If you have no plan to fly, or to have your own car, or don't like trains, it could be useful.

North of Penang is Langkawi, still one of the most romantic

areas in all Malaysia, mainly because of old legends connected with the island, but also because, to date, they have remained virtually unspoiled. There are hotels on Pekan Kuah so if you are set on seeing this charming area, you could find accommodation, but don't expect the luxury accommodation of Penang . . . not yet. The islands are ideal for those who want to get away from civilisation, but they have another kind of attraction for local people. Legend has it that if a woman bathes in the lake of Dayang Bunting island, or drinks its water, she will conceive. The story comes from long ago, when a Kedah princess was in love with a young commoner, but was forbidden by her family to marry him. They eloped to Langkawi, but the family wrath followed them, and in desperation the princess drowned herself in the lake. . . . In Malaysia there is always a story to match the haunting beauty of a place, though sometimes you have to search to find it.

Kedah is not spectacular. Most of it is flat, as behoves its role as a ricebowl State, and the road to Kuala Lumpur passes slurpy padi fields where the women work in the muddy waters and buffalo stand impassively as the heavy traffic thunders to the South. This is the only main road to Kuala Lumpur so take extra care. Malaysians are, for the most part, good drivers, but like anywhere else, there is always the chap who has come out of his kampong with his eyes shut and his feet on the accelerator. You could stop off for a well earned rest in Ipoh, the city of Tin in the Kinta Valley, and capital of Perak. The name of the town comes from the Ipoh tree (antriasis toximearia) which once grew in abundance. Aborigines still use the latex from the trees found in the jungle to make the poison for their darts, but there is only one tree left in Ipoh. If you wish to see it, go to the Seenivasagam Park. The town isn't very exciting, a mixture of old and new. The railway station is quite impressive, and there is the Birch Memorial, a clock tower erected in honour of the British Resident mentioned already.

More temples near Ipoh, this time of a most impressive variety. Indeed whether you approach the city from north or south you'll see the large limestone rock formations. The best is probably the one at Perak Tong, four miles south of Ipoh. It contains a 42 foot statue of the Sitting Buddha. Outside these temples are water lily pools and tortoise pools, and my thoughts went back again to the prisoner at Panching with no pool to sit by. . . . You can explore the Ipoh caves quite safely. Go behind the altars at Perak Tong and you'll find that there is a steep stairway which finally reaches an opening in the rock face some 300 feet above the ground. The view is wonderful on a clear day and it is worth the sweaty climb. If you can face it, another ascent will bring you to the painting of Kuan Yin. It all depends how much you require her good offices. Other caves are Sam Po Tong, where five monks and half a dozen nuns live in the cave and care for the thirty statues of Lord Buddha which can be found there. Wat Thai contains a Reclining Buddha, over eight feet long. It is supposed to have a fragment of Lord Buddha's bone within its head. You will notice that again and again, the name Thai comes up in these Northern States. The influence of Siam, stretches its fingers still into the present day in these religious and historical links, even though Malaysia has long outgrown the old relationship.

If you enjoy being seduced away from the main road southwards, an hour's drive from Ipoh will bring you to Lumut. From there is a brief journey to Pangkor, another island with a legendary princess, a resthouse, a hotel or two and bright green water which entices one to linger in its warm arms. At the time of writing, a new highway is to link Lumut with Kuala Lumpur via Telok Anson (of elephant fame) while from Penang, and taking the road via Taiping and Bruas, the distance is about 100 miles. The Tourist Corporations are no doubt busily engaged in thinking up schemes to expand the traffic to Pangkor. For my part, they can leave Paradise alone. It is enough for me that the island has the remains of an old fort bearing the coat of arms of the Dutch East India Company, which indicate that once it belonged to the Dutch. Later it became part of the Dindings, under British rule. At this moment, it belongs almost to itself. I can't help feeling that this is the way I want to remember it.

7. Enchanted Interlude

Land of the Hornbills . . . Land below the Wind . . . the two least-known of the Malaysian States are the ones which stretch the imagination, partly because of their very inaccessibility until quite recently to the average tourist traveller, but also because of the very name of the great slab of land on which they are perched. Borneo . . . headhunters . . . strange customs . . . unknown territory . . . it all tumbles into one's head at the mention of Sarawak and Sabah. They still are not exactly on the beaten track and it is necessary to make an effort to reach and traverse them, so it is unlikely that they will ever become the Costa Plasticas of South-East Asia, and I must admit to being selfishly grateful for that small modicum of comfort. Yet more people are finding their way to these states, in East Malaysia, and they are coming from Australia, USA and Europe to discover the sheer enchantment that lies within their hearts. This is not the easy tourist territory of Penang, K.L., Singapore or even the joyous East Coast. There is sophistication to be sure. Hotels, television, smart clubs, gold watches and fancy cars . . . to a point. But it is a veneer, and it wouldn't take very long for the first White Rajah of Sarawak to recognise his territory if he was awakened, along with Light and Raffles, for a looksee. As for Sabah, apart from its chaotic political situation which annoys even the most loyal admirers, it remains . . . Sabah. . . .

The comfortable winged chariot regularly provided by MAS for visitors to Sarawak brought me for my 'looksee' effortlessly over Kuching one Sunday morning in late March. The rains had been late, and the grey-green serpentine of the

Sarawak River looked replete below, as we made the final bow into Kuching airport. Again my thoughts reverted to Stamford Raffles, as they must do for any enquiring visitor to this South-East Asia area, for it was James Brooke's admiration of him, and the strong desire to emulate some of his feats, which led to the opening of Sarawak as it is today. Brooke, young, handsome elegant, with, we are told, an ability to charm a bird from a tree, had seen service in the Indian Army and after being wounded had fitted out a ship called the 'Royalist' and set off in search of adventure in South-East Asia. He arrived in the Sarawak River in 1839 and his advent coincided with a full-scale rebellion of the local Dyaks, Malays and Chinese against their rulers in Brunei. The overlords enlisted his reluctant help to quell the rebellion but after accomplishing this, he insisted that the rebels be allowed to return unmolested to their homes. With one deft stroke he brought peace to a warring land and made friends with both adversaries, a stroke which was rewarded by his election as Rajah of Sarawak by the Sultan of Brunei. The state was ruled from then on by a succession of White Rajahs of the Brooke family until it was passed to the British Crown on 14th May 1946 to become an autonomous state in the Federation of Malaysia. The name, Sarawak, is appropriate. It is a corruption of 'Serah Kapada awak', which means 'I give it to you'. Few people, other than those of Brooke's adventurous disposition, would have wanted it. It was, after all, a hazardous exercise even to get there, let alone to live there, before his time. . . .

Arrival at Kuching today is not without certain hazards either. The small airport is always in chaos on the arrival of the regular domestic MAS flights and it takes a major effort to struggle through the mass of bodies all intent on greeting friends and relatives from the 'mainland', to reach the luggage area, only to wait in the sticky heat, out of reach of the ceiling fans, while each piece of baggage is handled individually into the arrival area with far more care than that accorded to the sweating owners. Zaineb and I fought our way triumphantly out of the scrimmage and eventually found our hired car which was scheduled to take us into town. There aren't many

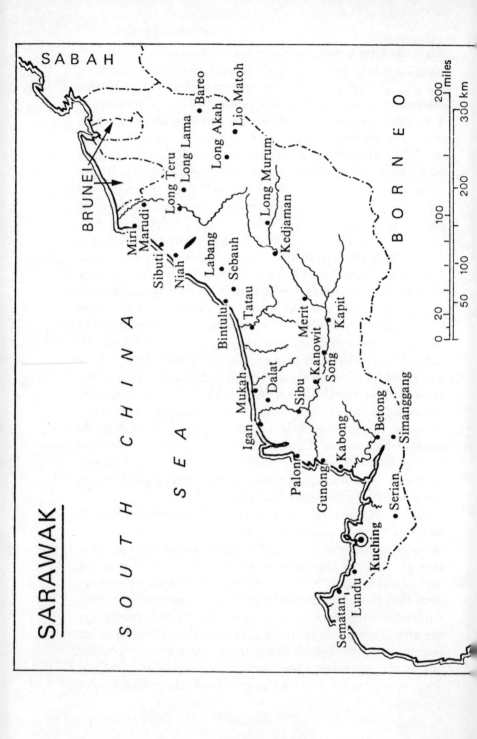

hotels in Kuching (although since my last visit the number has been increased by the long heralded opening of Holiday Inn), and rooms are always at a premium. We found ourselves deposited at a mouldering heap which would, in any other circumstance probably have qualified as something of a sailor's jolly, and for once, even I quailed. However, my cries of help down the telephone didn't go unanswered and Sir Galahad promptly arrived to succour the ladies in distress.

To be honest, no one else would have recognised the noble knight on his brave charger in disguise as Ambrose Wong in his Mercedes. . . . Ambrose is an energetic and utterly charming Chinese gentleman who took less than ten minutes to transfer us, baggage and all to his own small but spotlessly clean Borneo Hotel, which to us, at that moment was wearing the mantle of a five-star Sheraton. Ambrose looks in his late fifties, but admitted with a sly twinkle over an excellent dinner in the Mandarin Restaurant in Padungan Road that he was an unbelievable *eighty*. . . . When you go to Kuching, look him up. If he isn't wandering the world on his annual exodus, you'll invariably find him in his little office at the Borneo Hotel. He has more anecdotes on 'old Sarawak' and legends on haunted houses than I could possibly find room for in this book. He, and his many friends, are the real characters of Kuching. . . .

The town still bears the stamp of British rule in its neat Padang, the well-groomed lawns around the Istana, the wide tree-shaded streets and the superbly equipped Country Club where the comfortably-off citizens of all nationalities deem it necessary to have membership, but, down by the river, the town is all Orient. Shophouses huddle under their arcades and there are a multiplicity of hawker stalls beside the turgid river waters, selling every kind of fruit, nut and fish. It is virtually impossible for me to pass the fruit stalls in the East without purchasing, but there is one rule I keep. Buy only fruits with thick outer skins, such as lichees, oranges, bananas, pomeloes, durian, etc., and you can be fairly sure of avoiding Montezuma's (or Kuching!) revenge. . . .

You must forsake the congested area of Main Bazaar to visit

the building which I think is the most important reason for visiting Kuching, other than as a stepping-off place. The Sarawak Museum is one of the greatest gifts that anyone could have bestowed on this far-flung State, and it fell to Sir Charles Brooke, the second White Rajah, and nephew to James, to build and endow it. It opened in 1891 and at first sight it looks rather like the sort of manor house one finds in Northern France. This is not so far from the truth for it was designed by a Frenchman, one-time valet to Sir Charles. But, pause before you enter, to see the objects reposing on the lawn, and you'll feel the exoticism of Borneo closing around you. There is a burial pole there, made by Sekapans, and brought from Belaga in the upper Rejang. It is almost certain that it must have seen the sacrifice of many slaves at its foot. Look too at the strange figure carved in a large stone. This is a copy of a similar stone which still lies at the mouth of the Kuching River at Santubong, and which is at least 1000 years old. This land of the Hornbill was there, long before the White Rajahs came.

Inside, the museum is an ornately magnificent building divided into various ethnological sections and showing many facets of local tribal life. It is not strictly correct to refer to the Ibans as Sea and Land Dyaks. They were called Sea Dyaks by James Brooke because they went to sea with the pirates, but it is considered a little *infra dig.* today. 'We are not pirates,' they say, 'We are Iban. . . .' I made my way first to the East Gallery on the first floor, for there one finds one of the most important exhibits, in the form of a longhouse, and it gives one an excellent insight into the way of construction and the way of life, particularly useful if one intends to visit a longhouse in the interior of the country.

What is a longhouse? Broadly speaking, it is a whole village under one roof. There are sometimes a group of longhouses under one leader. Twenty or thirty families, often tied by relationship, live in a longhouse, which is a wooden and rotan building, raised on stilts above the ground, and entered by climbing a stairway of notched logs. The longhouse is usually divided into three parts, though designs do differ between Iban tribes (which we still can designate for our purposes as

Land and Sea Dyaks.' First comes a long communal room called the ruai. This is made of individual family sections, joined together, and occupies half the house. The other half is the walled-off sections belonging to each family, or Bilek. Outside the ruai, is a long open verandah or tanju, used for many purposes, such as drying padi, clothes and other activities. In the kitchen sections of each room are the household tools belonging to each family. In the museum some of the ancient bowls on show are of the type received in trading with Old China. Today, one finds plastic items used in their place. . . . Elsewhere in the museum, as well as within the longhouse exhibit, there are beautiful examples of Iban weaving. The patterns are exquisite and are surprisingly similar to those found among the Red Indians of North America. They say that, in the old days, the ambition of every Iban Man was to take a head in war and every Iban woman wished to weave a fine blanket to be used as an adornment for walls, a cover for a mattress when supplying a seat of honour, and so forth. On the door opening of some rooms in the exhibit are a row of human skulls. . . . Even in recent times, each longhouse had its own war party of able-bodied men, for there were frequent quarrels between longhouses, particularly between the Sea Dyaks and other Iban tribes, and in addition, it was the custom both with Land and Sea Dyaks that a young man should take a head, preferably in battle, but otherwise by any means he could – and it mattered not whether it was an old lady or a young child – before his sweetheart would even consider him for her husband. When someone was killed, the head was cut off with a parang, the long sharp curved knife, and borne home in triumph. At the longhouse it was welcomed by the women with great rejoicing, and should the longhouse be in a period of mourning the triumphant war cries automatically ended the sadness! The arrival of heads in a longhouse was celebrated by an 'enchaboharong' festival before the skulls were placed in positions of honour, to remain treasured possessions. The ones in the museum longhouse are held in little woven baskets, so be prepared for them. There is little variation in the types of clothing on display. Warriors were dressed in bark or skin coats and had strong rotan skullcaps decorated with hornbill feathers. Shoes were of wood, and often everything was elaborately decorated with patterns, human hair and with beads, for these last-mentioned have great importance, according to the colours, etc. I was intrigued by a notice which stood upon a small raised platform in the museum longhouse. It said, 'Bachelors of the longhouse and male visitors sleep on this raised platform, and in no circumstances should any decent young woman sit there. Those who do so are considered bad mannered, as well as a disgrace to their pareents.' Yet, as I knew, a young man may visit a young girl in her room. . . . An interesting distinction, in complete contrast to our own systems, even in today's changed world.

There is a particularly beautiful model of a Bersanding ceremonial chamber in the Museum. I have described Moslem wedding ceremonial elsewhere but if you are not lucky enough to see the real thing for yourself, and you are in the museum, this model really brings the whole ceremony alive for you. Another fascinating, if a little macabre, exhibit, is that of the coffins from the Kelabit burial ground in the uplands. These people keep a corpse for several years, usually on the verandah of the longhouse, contained in a wooden coffin with a bamboo stick judicially placed to drain the juices from the body. Then, when the body is quite dry, the bones are removed and placed in a pot. This custom is still observed among the Kelabit tribe, just as it was at Niah a thousand years ago. Niah. . . For the really dedicated anthropologist, geologist and botanist, surely Niah must be among the Meccas of their world. Any one of them visiting Sarawak would not rest until he has made the long and difficult journey to stand in the tremendous caves which lie halfway between Miri and Bintulu. For the rest of us, less enterprising mortals, and thanks to the great work of people like Tom Harrison whose recent and untimely death in Thailand wrote finis to a lifetime spent in the service of the Sarawak peoples, and their museum, we can see something of the caves in the display at that museum. There are superb representations of the long slow and painstaking work which is still being undertaken, and which has proved, beyond a shadow of doubt, that men walked the caves at Niah 40,000 years ago. The cast of the remains of one of them can also be seen too. The original rests where it was found. You can also see some of the bird's-nests from Niah. But they might put you off tasting the delicate soup into which these are made in many Chinese restaurants, which would be a pity. . . . Incidentally, if you do make the trip to Niah via the longboat, along the river from Batu Niah, and are staying at the bungalows or at the settlement longhouse, go to Sim's and ask them to prepare the soup for you, preferably before going on the trek to the caves. Stifle your qualms. It is superb. These days, fewer and fewer nest pickers wish to take up the trade. There are easier ways of making a living, than to clamber up bamboo poles 100 feet from the ground, in the darkness of the caves. You could go on to visit the Painted Cave, where the grave boats were found, but it is not an easy journey. Just remember that guides and permission *must* be obtained at the office of the Sarawak Museum in Kuching *before* going.

In the Museum, the book section provides some illuminating peeps into the past. There is a first-hand account of Borneo, written by an Englishman, Captain Daniel Beekman. It was issued in 1718 by a publishing house in Paternoster Row, London, and is obviously a very rare volume, containing an early map of Boreno which is accurate in many details. There are books from the Second World War which were written in the internment camps in the years up to 1943. Most of the pages are wrappings from tobacco, for paper was at a premium. But possibly the most important of all is the Deed of Cession, in James Brooke's own handwriting. It is hardly legible, but it mentions that a total sum of 6000 dollars was paid in 1861 for the countries which were to make up his 'Rajahdom'. And before you finally leave this fascinating and unique museum which must rank as one of the best in the world, taking a little while in the natural history section en route, spare a glance for the new State Crest. The land of the Hornbill has incorporated that bird into its coat of arms, together with a graceful hibiscus, the national flower of Malaysia.

Not very far from the museum is the Sarawak Arts Council souvenir shop crammed full on its upstairs floor with all sorts of irresistible items just crying to be taken home to every corner of the world. I found a delightful teakwood carving of an Iban on a dolphin, an exquisite silver belt of the kind that Iban women wear on special occasions, and a most interesting book by Hedda Morrison upon life in a longhouse. There were lots of other things I'd dearly love to have brought away but suitcases only stretch so far. Nothing was cheap, but considering the high standards of workmanship in most of them, prices were fair. It is worth looking in this store so that you can compare prices with others found in Kuching shops, as well as the quality. While on the subject of souvenir shopping in Sarawak and Sabah, don't leave it until you reach Sabah, except perhaps for something extra. Sarawak is more satisfactory and less expensive, though apart from items which are typically Iban, costs are generally higher than in Peninsular Malaysia.

One evening I was lucky enough to find a Wayang in full cry in the back streets of Kuching. A Wayang is a travelling Chinese Opera, beloved by Malaysians whether of Chinese origin or not, and may be found all over South-East Asia, usually playing one night stands. I've seen them in Singapore, K.L. and small villages in the countryside, and all of them have the sort of complicated plot which would do justice to Ben Travers and Mr. Punch. This one followed the normal patterns. Loud gongs, asides to the audience, and a general drifting in and out of characters dressed in gaudy satins and with most improbable make-up. These are traditional, but for me, this performance was enhanced by the presence of someone who I can only suppose to have been the stage manager. This gentleman, a minute Chinese dressed in blue shirt and disreputable slacks wandered about the set, a cigarette dangling permanently at the corner of his mouth, tidying cushions here sweeping unseen dust there, putting his sunglasses on and off, and completely ignored by all the actors. I know that in Chinese theatre stagehands are considered invisible, and obviously this one was no exception, but for me, the best moments of the evening came when he advanced to the front of the stage in the middle of what can only have been a most intense scene between hero and heroine and shooed a horde of kids off its flimsy apron. None of the audience seemd to mind, but perhaps this can partly be accounted for by the fact that the performance coincided with the Chinese Festival of the Tortoises and was taking place directly outside a small temple where celebrations were in full blast. Inside, the temple was in indescribable chaos, as crowds jostled with their burning joss-sticks from altar to altar, and others knelt among the discarded wrappings of offerings set upon long tables. There were beautifully decorated cooked ducks and chickens, fruit and a multitude of small cakes, made in the shape of tortoises, probably bought from the hawker stalls in the street outside.

There was one little lady who caught my eye. She was oblivious to the noise and smoke as she knelt in front of her special deity, shaking joss-sticks, and two curved stones. The idea seemed to be that one prayed, then threw the stones, and dependent upon which side the stone fell, the god's answer was given, probably as yes or no. The great advantage of this system would appear to be that one keeps on throwing and praying until the required replies are received, for, quite suddenly the devotee got up, bowed to the altar, picked up her bits and pieces including her decorated cooked chicken and departed. Indeed, this is a practical people. Nothing is ever wasted. And again I was struck by the completely free and easy attitude in the temple. I'd gone in, stood around, looking at everything and everyone, though keeping out of the way, and no-one seemed to mind that an unbeliever was present. It really is a most satisfactory sort of arrangement.

I waited with Zaineb on the steps of the Borneo Hotel early one morning in a state of considerable anticipation. This was the start of the promised journey to an up country longhouse and we were to stay in the village. Dunstan Lee, our guide, had told me that we were not going to the tourist longhouses along the Skrang River, but to another, less used to foreigners, and that in fact, I was to be their first European visitor. I'd dressed in jeans and stout shoes in preparation for the long jungle walk ahead of us, and my shirt was already sticking to my back, so I was thankful for once for the air-conditioning of the car. But once cooled off, we opened the windows and enjoyed the sweetness of the air as we took the road towards Serian. Out of Kuching the country is similar to Peninsular Malaysia, but there is an indefinable feeling that life is at a slower tempo here, and there were few people. Only an occasional dog was interested enought to bark as we passed. In Serian, we took breakfast in one of the open-fronted shophouse cafes, perching on tiny stools to partake of the excellent rice, washed down by cups of hot tea, made from teabags bearing 'Boh' labels, indicating that the tea came from the Malaysian Peninsula. In every town in Malaysia there are numbers of these cafes. They do look rather disreputable to European eyes, but the food is always freshly cooked, and tables usually clean, despite the cigarette butts on the stone floor. Don't be afraid to try them even though the ways are not yours. Other customers will accept you unquestioningly and with complete courtesy, for good manners are present in the humblest citizen. Perhaps that is one of the most enchanting things about going there. . . .

An hour or so later we pulled under the shade of a large tree on a country road where three children awaited. Dawa, our Iban driver, spoke to them. 'They are from the village and will carry our baggage.' 'Isn't it too heavy for them?' 'No, we have little and in any case they are used to it. Everything has to be carried to the village on this path.' The biggest boy produced an elongated wicker basket, loaded our belongings into it, hoisted it on to his back, and disappeared into the bushes followed by the smaller children. We followed, and found ourselves on a narrow dirt track.

The jungle is by no means a dark and silent place. Sunlight filters through in occasional patches, giving a greenish light eminently suitable for a Demon King. High tunnels formed by tall trees indicated a well-worn trail, most of it slightly uphill, and occasionally we broke out of jungle to cross open swampy ground where tree-trunks formed a balancing pole across the blue-black mud, and while the sweat poured from us, the atmosphere throbbed with life – the steady chatter of monkeys, the incessant chat of jungle birds and the constant sawing of crickets and a thousand nameless insects. Yet, we the human element and usually the most vocal, remained silent as we walked, and as I listen now to the recordings I made on that long hot hike, the only indication of our presence is an occasional heavy breathing as we paused to rest. We met some other people eventually, a man and a woman, heavily loaded with baskets of similar design to the one used by our boy porter, and Dawa exchanged comments with them. I could make out even fewer words than usual, for Iban Malay has many words of its own, and my knowledge of the language wasn't good enough to cope with that complication.

We were still straggling along the jungle path when a man overtook us, carrying an empty basket and calling a greeting as he disappeared ahead of us. As we came into a small clearing we saw the reason for his haste. He had crossed a perilous looking bridge across a fast flowing river, dumped his basket and plunged into the water to wash thoroughly before going home. This is apparently the normal process, for no-one ever loses an opportunity to remove the dust, and certainly, despite the heat and lack of sanitary facilities, there was never the stale odour of perspiration that one encounters so often among the great unwashed in many so-called civilised societies.

The group of longhouses nestled in a low valley between small hillocks, covered with pepper plantations and fruit and rubber trees. We were greeted by a company of cheerful children, a host of curious chickens and amiably barking dogs, two snorting pigs, and a group of bare-breasted young women whose red smiles betrayed early use of the betel nut. We climbed the perilous, notched steps to the first door, and following the example of my companions I removed my shoes before walking along the slatted platform. Groups of people, mostly women, children, and old men sat around, and apart from grave inclinations of the head, no-one took any notice as we were greeted by the welcoming committee. All but two of

the girls were naked to the waist, and children were completely so, but the men were so heavily tatooed in the most intricate
blue designs that it didn't even notice. The tattooes even
covered their throats. I was told later, and I can well believe it,
that the processes are extremely painful. The patterns are
applied with soot-covered wood, carved in the required
shapes, greased with pig fat and then driven into the skin by
taps on a sharp needle. Men do the work. I was also told that
if a man had taken heads, only his hands were tattooed, so of
course I kept a sharp lookout – after all, he might take a fancy
to my blonde head – but half disappointedly, I didn't see
anyone who qualified.

I shook hands all round, feeling that my lips were drawn
back into a permanently fixed smile as I received the
courteous and numerous greetings, and we were ushered
towards a beautifully embroidered rug, placed over cushions
on the floor. The wife of the headman, who is called in Iban
'bin tuai rumah' came forward with a large teakettle and cups,
and containers of rice wine. She was a greying little woman
with withered breasts, a tattoo on her forearm, and the longest
blackest fingernails I've ever seen. When we got to know each
other better, I discovered she was only in her forties. Life in a
longhouse isn't easy. We sat around for a while, surrounded
by dogs, fighting cocks tethered just beyond pecking distance
of each other, children and grown-ups, and from the noise
below, we were obviously sitting just above the abode of the
longhouses' pig population. People came and went. Dunstan
said this was all part of the ritual greeting but that in a while
we were expected to act as if we lived in the longhouse and no
notice would be taken of our presence. Sure enough when we
did depart to explore a little, and then came back to our base,
it was as if we were returning to a row of terrace houses with
each shut off completely from the others. Indeed in some ways
it was even more private, for no-one dreamed of 'peeking
through the curtains' . . . metaphorically speaking of course.
. . .

In the late afternoon, I was asked if I would like to go for a
bath with the ladies. Zaineb and I were provided with clean

sarongs into which we changed in the privacy of the family room where the women were engaged in preparing the evening meal. As everything takes place on the floor there wasn't much room between the heaps of rice on palm leaves, vegetables, pots, etc., all surrounding a smoky fire, but we managed, and set off to join the ladies at the river we had crossed earlier. Dunstan and Dawa had donned swimsuits and had come too. As our guides and caretakers they were under instructions to take care of us, and as far as they were concerned that included any sorties to the river. They stayed down stream of us, in courtesy, and the other women showed no resentment, so all was apparently well. The clear pale brown water was delicious as it rippled across our hot bodies where we sat on conveniently placed stones in the centre of the shallow stream, and we splashed happily, all sharing a large tablet of Lux soap, while remaining modestly under our sarongs. I was washing my hair when Dawa's voice came across the water. 'I see a snake.' 'Oh yes,' I said with my eyes shut, and continuing to rinse out the soap. 'You won't catch me as easily as that.' 'I can see a snake.' I opened my eyes, and sure enough one was swimming very fast in the shade of the far bank. I looked to the other women. They smiled and gestured for me to stand on a stone beside them, the snake slipped out of sight and was gone. We could, I felt, have been compared to a group of Victorian ladies looking at a mouse. We were quickly back in the water and continued our ablutions, but I didn't shut my eyes again!

Weaving and rice husking are only two of the many tasks of the Iban women. They also work in the plantations and padifields, as well as carrying out household tasks. I was shown the large bark containers set high in the rafters of the loft, reached on small versions of the notched ladders. The padi is stored in these for the entire longhouse. I noticed small hanging baskets beside them in the lofts, and was told that these were offerings to the spirits, for ghosts are part of the everyday life of Ibans in their capacity as spirit worshippers. All spirits, whether good or bad, have to be propitiated. There is some incursion of Christian and Moslem religions but life

changes slowly. Education though, is making some progress. I
met several very well educated young people living in 'my'
longhouse, and they told me that they make the long journey
to school daily. To walk all that way morning and evening and
to study, takes some effort. Many leave the longhouse to live
and work in the towns now, returning to the family home for
holiday periods, and the inevitable incursion of today's world
is in the longhouse. Linoleum takes the place of rush matting
in many bileks, transistor radios, wrist-watches and the inevitable plastic household items have their place, and on the
walls, official notices state when malarial spraying will take
place and pictures of the present King and Queen of Malaysia
and local film stars hang beside yellowing ones of the British
Royal Family. In the largish room behind the headman's
kitchen where we were invited to take supper, bedding was
piled in one corner, and evidences of peasant living were
around us, but there were modern clothes placed neatly on
wire coathangers, which obviously belonged to the young
members of the family. But there was a raised platform in
another corner, just as in the Museum. . . . Still not all look
upon change as progress. One old man told me, in passable
English, that he liked the reign of the White Rajahs best
because the cost of living was far too high now. Rice, he said,
cost ten times what it had cost in the old days for a katti
(about 2lbs), and it was all the fault of the Government, of
that he was quite certain. Not an unfamiliar cry in any country. . . . It was rather pleasant to notice that the old, whether
physically or mentally infirm, were being taken care of. There
was one old chap dressed in a filthy old loincloth, whose hair
hung in matted tangles and whose mind was wandering, who
was extremely happy to have his picture taken and was obviously fascinated by the guests. He was never pushed out of
the way – indeed, people made room for him. Elsewhere, old
people had their own corners and had people taking turns to
sit by them. Perhaps one has to go back to the more primitive
societies to find out how we, so-called sophisticates, should
behave.

When the tuai rumah, his sons and daughters, prepared a

special dancing display, the complainant about the Government was the chief performer in the drum and gong orchestra, and in tribute to his British listener, he wore a peaked cap which could have qualified him for British Railways. The display was particularly interesting because the family donned ornate traditional costumes. The particularly pretty women were loaded with silver, in the form of belts, wrapped around their sarongs. In addition, they wore silver necklets and earrings with brilliantly hued bead capes. I must add that, also in honour of my visit, the ladies wore white brassieres. . . .

The dancing is slow, graceful and stylised, and the posturised mime performed by the male dancers, resplendent in magnificent head-dresses of hornbill feathers, showed a man meeting an enemy, fighting him, and defeating him. Facing the threatening gestures and the spears, I was rather glad that they were all on my side. For the first time, I felt some sympathy for the Japanese troops with whom they had come in contact in the Second World War. Head hunting had virtually stopped by that time, but we were told, and I think with some truth, that it came back into full usage 'for the duration'. . . .

With the coming of evening, the fighting cocks were re-tethered outside and the dogs were banished while the population of all three longhouses crowded on to our verandah making a circle around us. Our small gifts of rice wine, cigarettes and potato crisps were passed around and everyone shared in them. In exchange I was offered a longhouse cigarette. I don't normally smoke, but I felt impelled to try in courtesy. The smoke was extremely hot, probably because the 'tobacco' is palm leaf. It also burned down very quickly. I took refuge in a small amount of rice wine. . . . After much giggling, young girls chose among the young men and invited them to dance. The custom is to show reluctance but to oblige, and inevitably, in due course, we, as the visitors had also to entertain the audience. Dancing to a gong and drum is not unlike a slow version of disco . . . and by remembering some of the movements performed during the afternoon display I didn't disgrace myself too much. When the social duties were over, we turned to community singing and here Zaineb came into her own. This had been her first sortie into Dyak territory, but she was au fait with all the popular Malaysian tunes from K.L. and soon had the girls and children crowding round to learn. The elders smiled and nodded and the young men pretended indifference, but I noticed they too were singing before long. The songs had a useful side too. Long after our departure, the songs would be sung and remind the longhouse of our visit. During the songs, Mrs Headman made me a present of a necklace of coloured beads, tasselled with a small bell. She draped it over my neck and then placed two narrow white bracelets on my arm, smiling her red-stained smile and saying something which translated, meant that I was now a member of the longhouse community and welcome any time. I reciprocated with a minute bottle of eau de cologne from my medicine store, and wished I had something more to give. When in Greece, two months later, I hit upon the very thing, and consequently, somewhere in the Sarawak jungle, there are several strings of blue worry beads now adorning the longhouse wall.

Gradually, the crowd thinned until Zaineb and I were the only ladies left and Mrs. Headman brought us fresh rush mats, light blankets and small pillows. I thought this would be the signal for the gentlemen to go, but still they sat on, silent for the most part, but talking sporadically and ignoring our presence. 'What do we do now,' whispered Zaineb. 'Let's lie down and see what happens.' She obediently lay down and immediately Mrs. Headman smiled and nodded, the men got up, and everyone departed, leaving us in complete possession of our part of the verandah, apart from a few dogs who lay near our feet. They'd taken the lamp too, so we were in complete darkness. But it was by no means silent. Now, as we lay on our mats, we could see the glow above the divisions between each section and could hear the conversations. These were not between the people occupying each room, but between households. It was like council flat tenants talking through the bedroom partitions. . . . I was just dropping off to sleep when there was the most almighty hubbub. Dawa, from his part of the verandah, shone a torch along the wall as a shadow slipped along it and a dog shook itself indiganantly. 'It is all right, said the reassuring voice, 'Someone has gone exploring and he trod on the dog.' No doubt the young man had made an assignation during the dancing. Where else can they meet except within the girl's part of her family room. The practice is an accepted part of life. After all, there is little else to do. Zaineb and I had quiet hysteria under our blankets, mosquitos bombed us, nameless insects shared our matting, the pigs, only an earbreadth away snorted peacably, and the dogs went back to sleep. Moments later, or so it seemed, a cock crowed in my ear. The fighting cocks were just outside our rotan wall and didn't know that it was the middle of the night. So much laughter necessitated a visit to the toilet. The only one for us consisted of an uninhabited longhouse room on another part of the tanju, so off we went, tripping over squawking chickens and praying we wouldn't fall through the unrepaired floors, which also served as our convenience. What the pigs thought I don't know.

The next arousal seemed minutes later but we had slept soundly and it was dawning. The longhouse inhabitants were starting their day, all talking at once, as dogs barked, chickens cackled and the cocks got the right time at last. We too, folded our mats and gratefully sipped the hot tea which arrived magically along with rice and eggs which Dunstan had prepared. All too soon, it was time to leave this happy place. I could better understand what James Brooke said in 1868. . . . 'If it pleases God to permit me to give a stamp to this country which shall last after I am no more, I shall have lived a life which Emperors might envy.' The enchantment of Sarawak had enveloped me too.

We stopped the car beside a waterfall on the homeward road, and donned our swim suits. A small frog shared his bathing place with me, and we sat companionably under the cool sweet waters for a long time. He, after all, had a greater right to be there than I.

Present day Sabah has literally jumped from the Stone Age into the 1970s. Traders from China found their way along its coasts centuries ago, taking treasures back to their Imperial

Majesty, and they called it the 'land below the wind', because in the calm waters they could find refuge from the monsoon storms. But they never ventured into the heart of the country. It would not have been very easy in any case, for the terrain is difficult, and even in the days when the country was known as British North Borneo, the hinterland was the domain of the jungle dwellers, such as the Muruts. Other tribes, such as Kadazans and Bajaus had their own ways too, the former were the farmers, the latter mostly seafarers, and the pattern has remained. But now there is a superimposition of modern political methods. It is a complication which makes Sabah a difficult land to recommend to the tourist, purely because political unrest does not make for the better type of tourism development to take place, but perhaps that will all sort itself out in time. South-East Asia usually makes its own way through its difficulties and shortcomings at its own speed, and one hopes that Sabah will be included in that. Getting into Sabah is a bit of a performance at the best of times. Immigration procedures are thorough even for other Malaysian nationals. At the time of a general election, when nerves were jumpy through local politicking, it was even more trying, particularly for a journalist, and despite my lack of interest in politics apart from their effect on tourism. By the time we finally put down at the airport at Kota Kinabalu, we had been all day in and out of the aircraft at various places, and I was about ready to return to Sarawak or K.L. Pride forbade that I should go all the way and turn back, but one look at KK and I wished that I had, for the city is one of the ugliest in South-East Asia. But let us look at the reasons.

Pirates knew the settlement and spent their time burning it down for years. When the British came to Borneo, they set up house on Gaya, the island in the bay, but during his rebellion against foreign rule, Mat Salleh destroyed that town in a surprise attack in 1897. When the Company rebuilt, it was back on the original site, naming it Jesselton after Sir Charles Jessel, but in 1945, this town was again destroyed, this time by bombing, so that, once more, after the Second World War, it was necessary to completely rebuild. Consequently there is nothing left of historic interest and the concrete used in the rebuilding doesn't make for architectural beauty. The town runs in a narrow strip under the shelter of a hillside in unimaginative lines, but later additions are far more attractive, particularly along Tanjong Aru, where the flowering shrubs and trees of the park are beautifully set against long backgrounds of casuarina trees and silver sand. And in Kampong Ayer, the water village, or up on Signal Hill, one does find sudden flashes of sheer beauty. Still, one can understand that when the State joined Malaysia in 1968 and was searching for a new name for Jesselton, they avoided the old Malay name which meant 'where the eye lingers'. . . .

I dropped my baggage at the Hotel and started to explore. Time was to be at a premium. I thought much better of KK after I had seen a sunset over Gaya Island from a point far along the harbour. It was one of the loveliest I have ever seen, shading the sky in tones of gilded apricot and reflecting in the water to my very feet. Long after it faded into dove grey I lingered, savouring the cool air before turning into the noisy streets of the city. By the time I got into the centre near the market place, I realised that this was rather a different place to anywhere else in Malaysia. Gone was the easygoing atmosphere of the East Coast, or the bustling importance of Kuala Lumpur and the sleepy charm of Sarawak. This was a busy place intent on its own business of buying and selling under the flaring lamps, and the traders still had the blaring modern American and British 'pop' tapes at full blast, but most of the stallholders didn't look like their kin a few hundred miles away and they smiled far less, though they were courteous. The answer was that most of the stallholders are refugees from the Philippines. They have no other home than their stalls and live upon them. One woman was setting out her sleeping mat among her wares as I bought a green coconut from her.

In the middle of the stalls, I found a medicine man, a common sight everywhere in South-East Asia. This one had a colleague and between them they kept up a patter which extolled the magical properties of a balm. The quack proceeded to demonstrate. He broke a bottle and chewed its pieces, 'losing his voice' in the process. After applying the balm, and swallowing a few drops, his voice came back. A spectator came forward to have some of the product applied to his leg, which he claimed he couldn't bend. After the ministration of the magic ointment, he still couldn't bend it, but on assurance from the medicine men, he nodded, and was swallowed up into the night while the believers crowded round, anxious for more miracles and free shows. I left them all to it eventually, but I held on to my wallet whilst there. It all reminded me so much of Petticoat Lane. . . .

I had intended to have dinner in the restaurant at the hotel, but one look at the tables told me this was no place for me. Most had the unmistakable air of rendezvous, and not between men and women known to each other. I ate at a small and excellent Indian restaurant in the main street and went to bed early. The air, coming straight from the sea, was fresh and cool, and the town was remarkably quiet, so for once I woke refreshed, rather than in that hated air-conditioning.

My morning started at 5.30 as we made for Kota Belud in order to arrive at the tamu, or market. Once out of Kota Kinabalu, the scenery starts to come into its own, and it too, is quite different to anywhere else. Within an hour the hills appear, blue violet and smokey green in the morning light, and suddenly Mount Kinabalu rises straight from a plain. The highest mountain in South-East Asia, its 13,000 feet has a revered place in the religions of the local people for they consider it to be the resting place of the spirits. When one sees it putting on its daily garb of fleecy white, and hiding its head from view, it isn't hard to understand why. If you go along this road, take your photographs the minute you see the mountain. It won't be available for interview later in the day.

The market at Kota Belud is a colourful affair with Bajau women sitting in the shade of the trees with their wares spread before them and their heads protected by folded cloths. Some sell doughnuts or odd looking cakes, others fruit and vegetables, and yet others had smelly heaps of tiny fish and small crabs, on which the flies were having a field day. I was

surprised to see the fish. At that time Sabah coasts were suffering from pollution from a gelatinous plankton and I had been
warned not to swim or eat fish temporarily. But these fish
were from the rivers. They still didn't look that good to me. By
now the dangers will have passed and the Bajaus will be back
at their main occupation as fishermen. They are also good
horsemen, and if rumour is to be believed have a reputation as
pirates. Nothing surprises me in Sabah. It is such a mixture of
fact and fiction that anything is possible.

I have not yet been to the top of Mount Kinabalu. There
must, after all be something to go back for. But if the surrounding scenery is anything to go by, it would be a magnificent
sight. Apparently, to see that vista stretching before one, after
the gasping way to the summit with local guides, one must
spend the night at a hut, in order to accomplish the last
stretch in the early morning before the mountain has time to
don its shroud. The National Park is very lovely, and there are
rest cabins and huts available, but you must book well ahead
to stay in one. Further on is the Orang Utan Sanctuary at
Sepilok not far from Sandakan. Lack of space forbids that I go
into details about it, and in any case, so much has been
written and filmed about the threatened extinction of this
magnificent and harmless inhabitant of the forest by far more
qualified commentators than I. In my opinion this place is a
must for anyone who takes the trouble to go to Sabah, for such
a visitor would care deeply about natural habitats and the
creatures who dwell in them. This Sanctuary has done a great
deal already to protect orangs, caring for orphaned little ones
and trying to equip the majority for life in the wild. Some
never go back. They discover the delights of the Welfare State
and like their sophisticated existence. Who can blame them.
They, after all, are only emulating some of their human
brothers in living on handouts rather than fending for themselves.

From Sandakan, if you have the time, hire a Land-Rover
and go to Gomantong Hill. The limestone caves are covered
with the type of edible bird's-nests also found in Niah. It isn't
so spectacular, but is slightly more accessible. Finally, on a

small island offshore at Sandakan, there is a colony of green turtles. They, too, have a timelock ticking away their existence. All Sabah needs time. Time to settle its political differences. Time to build itself into a cohesive whole, time to be seen, explored and appreciated. All this *takes* time, and it remains to be seen just how much is available to the people and animals who live in the Land below the Wind.

8. Island City: Singapore

While in Singapore in February 1976 I bought a long-coveted and rather expensive camera in a store in North Bridge Road (I should add immediately that British Customs exacted their dues when I returned to the U.K!). Precious package in hand, I walked back along the verandahed street, into High Street, crossed through the circling traffic, past the elderly facade of the Singapore Cricket Club where a small army of 'boys' were cleaning the cars of the Singapore-born 'tuans' as they had done for generations when the British were there and over to Queen Elizabeth Walk to the point where it meets the bridge across the mouth of Singapore River. The Walk has long been a popular evening parade, but during the day there are few people and most of these seek the shade of the trees along its length. I too found an empty bench out of the reach of the fierce sun and proceeded to examine my new toy, longing to put it into service. I looked around for something on which to focus it, and my eye fell upon one of Singapore's recent acquisitions. The Merlion is the symbol of the industrious Tourist Promotion Board which is doing so much to bring Singapore's holiday image to the notice of the travelling millions, and is supposed to represent that strange creature which gave its name to the Lion City ... Singapura. Its sightless eyes gaze ever seawards as the sampans pass uncaringly below, but from its mouth flows an incessant stream of water, and it reminded me that water was one of the reasons for the foundation of Singapore as a port of call in Raffles's day. So I left my seat in the shade and after pausing for a welcome cup of tea at the Polar Cafe in High Street, where the same family has run the business for 50 years and make the best curry puffs in Singapore! I set out to walk the length of Coleman Street to the spot where the Armenian Church stands near the junction of Hill Street and Canning Rise.

From there it is an uphill breathless walk in the heat to Fort Canning, where a royal palace once crowned the summit. Long ago the hillside was thickly wooded and there was a fresh clean stream in which the royal ladies could bathe. The area was strictly forbidden to the ordinary mortals dwelling at the foot of the rise, and when Raffles came, centuries later, he learned that the hill was still known as Bukit Larangan, For-bidden Hill. The water from the Forbidden Stream was in all probability among the first that the investigating shore party found, although the main water that they discovered was Fresh Water Stream which lay further over from Bukit Larangan. So it is a nice idea to start one's musings and perambulations around the city from here. After all, one of the most pleasing things for a Westerner about Singapore is the knowledge that water on the entire island is good, sweet and quite safe to drink without boiling. The 'winter' months presented some problems in early 1976 because of the long drought months, and levels of reservoirs reached very low points, necessitating the procurement of even more supplies from Johore, but water is always pure. The only reason for carafes and thermos-flasks in hotel bedrooms is to keep it cool. In most homes in Singapore the 'cold' tap gives tepid and even quite hot water, but it happens all the time there, and one keeps bottles of drinking water in the fridge.

On Bukit Larangan there used to be a cemetery. 'I can't think what you always find so interesting about cemeteries,' is a comment which has been used many times to me. Yet they give so much information on the past in their simple inscrip-tions and by spending just a few moments looking at the names of those who have long since gone from human sight, one finds very many clues to time gone by, and frequently, can start off along a whole new train of exploration. Fort Canning cemetery is a case in point. The ancient royal families had placed their burial grounds on the side of the hill, a common

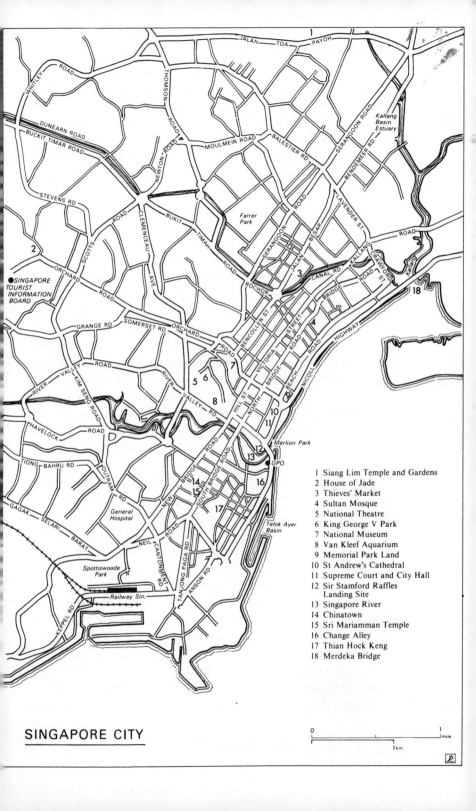

1 Siang Lim Temple and Gardens
2 House of Jade
3 Thieves' Market
4 Sultan Mosque
5 National Theatre
6 King George V Park
7 National Museum
8 Van Kleef Aquarium
9 Memorial Park Land
10 St Andrew's Cathedral
11 Supreme Court and City Hall
12 Sir Stamford Raffles
   Landing Site
13 Singapore River
14 Chinatown
15 Sri Mariamman Temple
16 Change Alley
17 Thian Hock Keng
18 Merdeka Bridge

SINGAPORE CITY

0   1 mile

1 km

occurrence in the east. Cemeteries, particularly Chinese ones are built wherever possible on rising ground in order to protect them from landslides, floods, animal depredation, robbery, etc. The higher the position, the better off the family of the deceased seems to be the rule. Raffles decided to build his own house on Bukit Larangan, commenting in a letter that 'if his bones were to stay in the East they would mix with the ashes of Malayan kings' and his bungalow of wood and at-tap, built in two weeks, was placed immediately above the Christian cemetery which had also been established. But Raffles wasn't too happy with that. If one is uncharitable one might think it spoiled his view. . . . Anyway, he commented that, 'The present European burying ground is too restricted and otherwise objectionable,' and he ordered its removal. Lieutenant Jackson, the Executive Engineer complied with the order, and the cemetery was moved to its present position. After that time, Bukit Larangan became Government Hill to the settlers, and it remained under that name until after the Indian Mutiny when Singapore was having a fit of the jitters and it was decided to give the settlement some military protection. Government Hill received a fortress and guns and was renamed Fort Canning, after the Right Honourable Viscount Canning, Governor General of India in 1856-62, and has retained that name ever since.

The view in those days must indeed have been splendid. One could have seen across Sepoy Lines, Hill Street, which is the oldest thoroughfare in Singapore and right across to the Padang and to the sea. Now, alas, much is hidden by the buildings which crowd in on one, but the area is rich in history. Few people realise that Raffles was intensely interested in all forms of science and even fewer realise that it was he who founded the London Zoo on his return from the East. He started the Singápore Botanical Gardens too, but they were not on their present site in his day. They abutted on to Hill Street, just below Government Hill and were under the charge of Dr Nathaniael Wallich. On this site is the Armenian Church mentioned previously, the oldest religious building in Singapore. There were 12 Armenian families in Singapore from its inception and the community remains today as one of the most respected in the whole of South-East Asia. The church was commissioned by the original settlers, among them the Sarkies family, and the plans were drawn up by George Drumgold Coleman, who had come to Singapore in 1826 to be Superintendent of Public Works and Land Surveyor after considerable experience in Calcutta and Batavia. He built a great deal of old Singapore, though sadly, very little of his work remains today. There is one example, built into the Convent of Holy Jesus, and many old sketches and paintings show others. He built the original Raffles Institute demolished only in 1973 when the school was transferred elsewhere in the city, many merchants' houses, including the one incorporated into the Legislative Assembly building, and the first St Andrew's Cathedral, which was a twin to the Armenian Church.

Coleman received 400 Singapore dollars for his work on the Armenian Church, which was hardly a fortune, and it was built in 1835-6. It is dedicated to St Gregory and the interior is built in a circle, with a semi-circular chancel on the East. Four small corner chambers make the building into a square. There are Doric porticoes and a balustrade and originally there was a high dome and a bell tower, but these became unsafe, and were replaced with the present little spire. The Armenian Church was, also, the first in Singapore to install electricity, which I suppose is some sort of tribute to its Church Council. Coleman's name lives on, not only in 'his' street, but in the bridge between Hill Street and New Bridge Road. He died of fever in Singapore in 1844, and is buried in Fort Canning cemetery. Not far from his grave, there is a little area devoted to the D'Almeida family. Dr José d'Almeida was a Portuguese surgeon who set up as a merchant, had several wives and 20 children, whose descendants still live in Singapore today. But his main claim to fame is the fact that he was responsible for sending samples of gutta-percha the forerunner of rubber, back to London and so could have been said to be one of those who planted the first idea of the usefulness of rubber in the minds of men.

On the far side of Fort Canning is the floral clock on Clemenceau Avenue, in King George V Park. In the grounds of the park is a startling new building which houses the National Theatre, but in addition you will find the Van Kleef Aquarium. There are all kinds of delightful inhabitants here, such as seahorses, brilliant corals, and many charming little tropical fishes found in local seas, (there are a number of shops specialising in these in Selegie Road, just beyond the Cathay building, which might be of interest to aquarists). There is however, one inmate in the Van Kleef that one could well do without. This is the deadly little sea snake. It looks like a ribbon of seaweed, is found in deeper waters off Malaysian coats, and has killed a number of hapless fishermen in its time for there was no known antidote.

Less menacing are the contents of the National Museum on Stamford Road, along the other side of Fort Canning. This was the old Raffles Museum established in 1832, but has been completely refurbished and looks very elegant now. It contains an excellent collection of South-East Asian art, but more interesting to the would-be historian are the fine collection of prints and sketches of Singaporeana. Very good copies of these are on sale and are easily carried souvenirs of a sojourn in the Lion City.

Further on from the Museum is the junction of Stamford Road with Orchard Road. There is an elderly, rather ramshackle looking building here, bearing the notice that it is the Y.M.C.A. Look well at it and give it some respect as you pass, for the sake of the many people who suffered and died within its walls at the hands of the Kampetai (the Secret Police) during the Second World War. Among the many who were held there before imprisonment elsewhere was the then Bishop of Singapore, 'Jumbo' Wilson, who for so many years afterwards, conducted the annual Remembrance Service in the Albert Hall. Local people said that the screams from the Y.M.C.A could be heard at the top of the Cathay building on the corner of Mount Sophia. One has to cross Dhoby Gaut to get to Cathay, and here again there are small fragments of history. Dhoby Gaut was, as its name implies, the place where the Indians did all their washing in the clean sweet water which ran there, and Mount Sophia, originally known as Bukit Selegi, once held the house of a Captain and Mrs. Flint. This lady was the sister of Sir Stamford Raffles and the hill was renamed in honour of his wife, Lady Raffles. When Cathay Building was erected in 1937–9, it towered over the entire area of Orchard Road, but now the forest of hotels which line the upper reaches make the old 'skyscraper' look like an undernourished midget. This is the main artery of Tourist City, and the majority of visitors spend their sleeping hours and a goodly proportion of their waking ones, in its vicinity. There are many shops here, most of them long established and reputable, but we won't stop to shop now. Once embroiled in the frenzy of souvenir shopping in Singapore there is little time for anything else.

Hotels in Singapore are almost universally excellent and although it is highly pleasurable to live in luxury surroundings, it is not necessarily mandatory to choose the most expensive in order to enjoy one's stay. There are high standards of cleanliness in all of them, so, as in so much else in life, much depends on personal requirement. While there are many more luxurious and modern hotels, I still think that the title of doyen must go to Raffles. Immortalized, satirised, and patronised by the famous and infamous, it is still the target for many visitors who feel that there is just nowhere else to stay, or for those who at least want to have a drink there to savour the yesterday atmosphere. It was, and it still is, a very pleasant oasis, and I for one was pleased to be reassured very recently that there was no intention of tearing it down despite reports to the contrary. A great many people would grieve if that sad day came to pass – and not all of them would be Europeans.

Even in the 'new' Singapore industry of tourism and hotels, one can find little snippets of the past. For instance, within twelve years of the founding of the Colony, there was a boarding house on High Street, run by a Mr. Hallpike. When George Coleman, the architect, left his house at No. 3, Coleman Street, to go back to Ireland on long leave in July

1841, it was turned into the 'London Hotel' by a gentleman
who bore a French name, Gaston Dutronquoy, though it turned out he was from Jersey. I presume that he must have moved
when Coleman came back to the Colony, but in any event it is
recorded that he moved his hotel to the Esplanade, where it
was regarded as the 'best hotel in town'. There were two
two-storeyed buildings, converted from private houses, which
faced the sea, and the charge for a single room with breakfast
and dinner at a public table was one dollar fifty cents per day.
Private sitting-rooms cost more. There was an extra charge for
baths taken in a separate block from the hotel, and this was
considered to be extortionate by one visitor who says that 'it
was unreasonable seeing that water was abundant and close
to hand.' By 1852, there was another boarding house, run by a
Mrs. Roberts, also in Coleman Street, on a site later occupied
by the Adelphi Hotel until its recent demolition. We're told
the food in Mrs. Roberts day wasn't particularly good. That
fault could not have been laid at the door of the now defunct
Adelphi, nor indeed to most hotels in Singapore at the present
day, where menus are invariably good. But to eat cheaply, you
must visit the tiny eating stalls. These are rigorously inspected
by the Health Authorities, so one is safe with most of them.
The ones used by foreigners, and therefore slightly more expensive are those which make their appearance nightly in
Orchard Road Car Park. During the day, when the Car Park
has its mechanical occupants, try the avenues of tiny eating
houses behind the market just across the road. The food is excellent. The last time I was there I had magnificent turtle
soup, boiled mee, bean curd and coconut juice for about 50
new pence. Surroundings aren't the Ritz, but it is all part of
the atmosphere. Another excellent place for lunch is the old
Telok Ayer market just off Raffles Quay. This building was
one of the main markets in Singapore, but now has been
cleaned up and is the daily venue for about a hundred eating
stalls with Chinese, Indian, Malay and Nonya dishes as well
as the odd hot dog or two. It is patronised mostly by people
from surrounding office blocks, and supplies some of the best
lunchtime value in Singapore. Of course, if you don't like sit-

ting on a three-legged stool in the Chinese equivalent of
Bedlam, transfer your affections to the more elegant surroundings of Hin's heavenly cookhouse at the top of the Singapore
Hilton, where the food and the view are out of this world (with
prices to match) or Omar Khayam, or for local Nonya food,
Lune Coffee Shop. In the evening try Albert Street, particularly Fatty's. He's been there for ten years or more. Others are
almost as good nearby, or you could go out to Katong stalls for
seafood. Where does one even begin to stop on the subject of
food in Singapore?

In Bugis Street, the food is fair, but the girls are fairer, and
it comes as a bit of a shock to realise that they are all
transvestites. If you accept the scene, and want to see for
yourself, don't go before 1 am.; the 'girls' don't appear much
before that. But Singapore wouldn't be the same without
them, so say goodbye to your beauty sleep and go. . . .

From Orchard Road hotels there are several interesting
short excursions if time is limited. On Wednesday evenings try
the Pasar Malam (Night Market) in Tanglin Road. It is about
a ten minute walk from Ming Court Hotel corner, and is
rather like Portobello Road with its hurricane lamps and gar-
ish colouring. But here you'll find Chinese and Indian traders
and Nepalese too, so business must have looked up in the last
few years. They wear smart clean shirts these days and good
wrist-watches, all very different from the rags one used to see.
They have trays of the usual assortment of cheap stones, but
when I asked one of them if he had any real turquoise matrix,
he unrolled a well-worn black cloth and showed me an exquisite piece which would have matched very well with stones
I had bought from his brethren years before . . . but to get to
the price I had wanted to pay then, it had taken two weeks of
daily hard haggling, and I had no such time to spare on this
trip. Half the fun at the Pasar Malam comes from watching
the crowds as well as the stallholders. All Australia seemed to
be on the lookout for bargains and the humour was all very
gregarious and jolly. Pasar Malam is on every evening of the
week somewhere in Singapore, so if you miss out at Tanglin,
get a list of possible stopping sites from the Tourist Promotion

Board Office in Tanglin Road.

Walking back towards the hotels, with traffic passing occasionally, you may hear the crickets chirping incessantly in the casuarinas, and it reminds that it is not so long ago that this area was all countryside. Only 100 years ago it was the edge of the jungle, where tigers lurked ... and there were plantations here too, including one owned by a George Nicol (no relation as far as I can discover), which grew nutmegs. Look for these in the Botanic Gardens, so that you will know what to buy if you see them on a street fruit stall; the fruit resembles a pale peach. While we only know the kernel as a spice, the Chinese eat the fleshy part which draws the mouth slightly and leaves it refreshed. You can also buy it grated into thin slices like coconut.

Not far from the junction of Clemenceau Avenue and Orchard Road is the entrance to the Istana. This was the Government House of Colonial Days and is now the ceremonial home of the President of the Republic of Singapore. It is a most beautiful house and must have cost a pretty penny when it was built under the direction of the Colonial Engineer, Major McNair, for occupation by Governor Harry St. George Ord, CB. Ord was Governor for six years, between 1867 and 1873 and until the house was ready in 1869, he lived, as his predecessor had done in a house atop Leonie Hill. The old house disappeared long ago and for some years the grounds were occupied by several blocks of very pleasant and very cool flats. I can vouch for them, for I lived there myself for nearly two years. But they, in their turn have disappeared in readiness for highrise buildings.

Governor Ord was undoubtedly an extravagant Governor, and reputedly a highly unpopular one, but at least the house today remains one of the loveliest in Singapore and the rightful setting for the men who, in the name of Britain, and now Singapore as a nation, have settled destinies over the years. I was lucky enough to visit the house on several occasions. One of them was for a meeting of the Corona Society, an organisation composed mainly of expatriate women. It was in early '59, and it was late on an intensely hot afternoon. We sat on little chairs in a cool, high-ceilinged room, listening to the speeches and presentations and looking out on the truly immaculate gardens, and I remember thinking that, for a few moments of time, I was part of the sunset over the British Empire. I thought too how quietly and gently it was happening. In another country, in another age, I might have been on my way to the guillotine. Perhaps we owe far more than we shall ever know to the patience, wisdom and understanding, not just of the Europeans who helped to make Singapore great, but to the generations of Asians who worked with and alongside them.

Try to find time to visit the House of Jade. To do so, you will have to obtain a pass from Haw Par Bros Limited, 3B Lim Teck Kim Road. This is not difficult. Just tell them the day you want to visit and it will be freely given. The house was built nearly fifty years ago for the Aw brothers, and is the white house standing behind the green one at the corner of Tanglin and Nassim Roads opposite the entrance to Ming Court Hotel. The Aw Brothers were Boon Haw, (meaning Tiger) and Boon Par (meaning Lion) and came from Shanghai. They were the founders of a business which dealt in a cure-all balm, known throughout China, and eventually all Asia with Singapore as its headquarters, as Tiger Balm. It comes in little jars, both tiny and large, and resembles Vick's Vapour Rub. . . . It is universally used for headaches, toothaches, rheumatism, sore throats, etc., and I must admit that I always have a jar stashed away in the house. Perhaps faith is the real cure-all, but whatever it is, it works as far as I am concerned.

The Aw Brothers became tremendously wealthy and Boon Haw began collecting jade and other precious stone carvings about forty years ago. Jade has always been associated with China, and the earliest examples of Chinese carving of the stone are on nephrite from the Sinkiang region. It was used for the carving of ritual objects, such as birds, fishes, etc., and the art reached its peak at the end of the Chou dynasty and in the Jan dynasty (206 B.C. to 220 A.D.) when the carvers made intricately linked pieces fashioned from a solid piece of jade. The stone was supposed to have healing and calming properties as well as being credited with the power to repel evil. Modern Chinese are not quite so superstitious as their elders, but still one sees many Chinese women wearing rings and earrings fashioned from jade and from jadeite, which comes from Burma.

Some of the pieces in the collection date back to the Ch'ien Lung period, and there are two jadeite discs showing the Queen of the Western Heaven, Hsi Wang Yu. There is also a table screen which is worth seeing, and several lovely statuettes of Kwan Yin, Goddess of Mercy, in jade, agate and rose-quartz. There are some particularly beautiful pieces of this last-mentioned stone, fashioned into phoenix and peony shapes. This stone, found all over the Far East in curio shops, actually came into China from America and much jade also comes from that country. The Phoenixes . . . or should it be phoenii . . . were carved in the late 19th century so they are not particularly ancient by Eastern standards. Most of this collection comes from around the same period, but I am told that the items are unique of their kind. To me this isn't particularly important, for it is the sheer beauty of the carvings which takes me back to the House of Jade. It certainly isn't the lighting, or indeed the method of display, both of which are very poor, and I long to take the whole place in hand. . . . But Mr. Boon Haw and Mr. Boon Par look down rather forbiddingly from their wall mountings so I go back into the hot sunshine and forget about good intentions until the next visit.

The Botanic Gardens are also within easy reach of Orchard Road hotels, and a taxi will get you there in about five minutes, along Tanglin Road and Napier Road to its junction with Cluny Road. Go in the early evening, before the quick dusk, when it is cool enough to walk. Until very recently the Botanic Gardens were enlivened by the antics of several families of small monkeys who descended on the unwary, snatching handbags, cameras, toys, etc., and from a safe distance up a tree, proceeded to tear them to pieces in front of the helpless and indignant owners. The monkeys were harmless enough, in the beginning, but then through the sheer stupidity of their human visitors, they formed the habit of biting and the edict went out . . . destroy them. A Chinese friend of mine said that it had been rather a sad business, as they had been first starved out, then shot. The price of progress? . . .

I was happier with the disappearance of the packs of mangy dogs and scraggy bent-tailed cats. These were a distressing feature of life, to say nothing of a health hazard, and in the general facelift that Singapore has undergone, they too were rounded up and destroyed. But I miss the monkeys. The swans are not nearly so entertaining. An Indian professor I know summed it all up for me. 'You see,' he said, 'it wasn't the children. They understood the monkeys. It was their elders who tormented. In my view we must educate the humans and not the animals. So the next generation will have a chance of restoring the balance.'

Monkeys or not, Singaporeans like to stroll in the Botanical Gardens and there are few pleasanter ways of spending an hour. There are thousands of tropical plants in perfect condition, and a wilderness of orchids which are after all, Singapore's national flower. I never cared much for these before living in the East, for there is something predatory about them. The illusion still lingers, though I have come to admire their myriad exquisite forms. One can buy orchids very cheaply in florists and markets and unlike other tropical blooms they last well in water. One can have them sent to any part of the world at reasonable cost. Go and admire and make a note of varieties in the Botanic Gardens, and then see what the florists can produce. Indoor gardeners in Britain would be quite discouraged if they visited the many nurseries which still ply down the middle of the Bukit Timah Road (ground has been taken for roads on either side of them). They would find all the little plants they cherish at home so carefully, growing quite happily in the open air and ten times as large – anthurium, shrimp plants, rubber plants, colaeus . . . but discouraged or not, if there is time, do go and see for yourself.

I am never sure which is the better time to go to Mount Faber. At sunset, the thunderheads build up across the islands to produce purple, crimson and flame stage effects. At night, a velvet sky caresses with a warm finger and the moon hangs low enough to touch beyond the island, enticing one's eyes away from the man-made illuminations of the city behind. I guess it depends entirely on mood, and to an extent upon one's company too. You could of course have a little of both scenic delights by going in time for the sunset and staying on until the last glow has gone and the stars have arrived. Mount Faber has always been a pleasant spot, and until the opening of the cable car to Sentosa (Blaku Mati) comparatively isolated, beloved best by lovers and solitaries. Now there is a constant coming and going to the cable car station during the day, but at sundown it comes into its rightful own. Try it one evening. You won't forget it.

There is also a magic when you go to catch the cable car by day, but it is a different sort. It is fun swinging out across the Singapore Roads, seeing the green seas streaked with ochre where the rivers join it and ships lay, like toys near Jardine steps. Then the car arrives with a little hiccup at the island terminal and there is the inevitable soft drink stand. Fraser and Neave have been selling soft drinks in Singapore since 1883. Before that, believe it or not, Mr Fraser and Mr Neave ran a printing works they bought from Missionaries. Odd to think that the ever popular Green Spot soft drink came from a well-meaning effort to convert the Malays to Christianity! I shall always have a soft spot for Sentosa though it has changed greatly. It used to be a favourite picnic spot for those of us who were lucky enough to have small boats and has seen many a Boxing Day picinic when the kids played in the shallows inside the safety of the coral reef, while we ate cold turkey and drank Tiger Beer in the shade of the palms, thought of our folks back home, and never saw another soul all day. . . .

Sentosa's small population had lived there for generations undisturbed by the fortifications and a transient military who manned them. Now the military are gone and locals are being transferred slowly, reluctantly, to the 'mainland' of Singapore while the island is undergoing transformation into a holiday centre with hotels, cottages, restaurants, shopping plaza and other trimmings seemingly inseparable from the conception of tourism. There is a new Golf Club there now too. I visited it one afternoon during the rainy season. It rivals, and surpasses many I've seen elsewhere. Splendid greens stretching away to the sea, a luxurious club-house where it is all too obvious that its membership list includes many of the most influential people in Singapore and for the guest holiday members who will undoubtedly go there. I'm not sure that it *is* an improvement really – certainly not for the people who considered the island as home before the invasion of their world.

There is an interesting and well presented coralarium on Sentosa. An open bus with bamboo 'chicks' ineffectively keeping out the rain, in the 'care' of an exceedingly grumpy driver, jerked us round the little roads to reach it. In the gardens at the Coralarium Malay women gardeners were working with the age old tools of parang and chongkol to keep the rapid tropical growth in check. They didn't mind a bit when I photographed them, though they were inclined to pose, leaning on their hoes in the manner of labourers the world over, which rather spoiled the effect. Bathing beaches are enclosed now in a lagoon, and it didn't *look* spoiled. Let's hope it stays that way. You can visit Sentosa as part of a harbour cruise, or retrack across to Singapore by cable car, watching Pulau Brani fan out on your right as the skyscrapers come back into perspective, or you can wait for the small ferry which goes back to Jardine Steps. Instant Asia was, until 1976, quite near at hand, but now it is being transferred into a complex behind Tanglin Road, in order to be more accessible to the tourist district. Instant Asia! What a horrible title to give a show!! I went to see what it was all about. Briefly this is a small but very colourful presentation of some of the traditional music, dances and entertainments that form part of the way of life of the multi-racial society of Singapore. Few people are lucky enough to see many of the colourful spectacles that Singapore can present free of charge almost any day of the week in her streets and temples, mainly because few people know exactly where they are going to be and, in any case, dancing and music are often spontaneous things. Consequently the Tourist Board have assembled a selection of the most famous entertainments from Chinese, Malay and Indian cultures. It is an unpretentious uncomplicated performance, and not, thank heaven, nearly as 'touristy' as some I have seen in other lands, and it nearly always includes certain of the more popular offerings. Ronggeng, or Joget for instance are the Malay dances in which the couple dance in rhythm but never touch. Liven it up to modern music and it could pass for the more frenetic disco style, but it is much more graceful and is not nearly so easy as it looks. The Chinese always produce a dragon which is enormous fun, but the highspot is, without exception, always the snake charmers. Time was when one could always find these gentlemen ensconced in the shade of the green between St. Andrew's Cathedral and the Adelphi Hotel of happy memory, but on this trip I had searched for them in vain. When I got to Pasir Panjang, there they were in force at Instant Asia, and no doubt will be transferred by now to Tanglin Road or thereabouts. The spectacle of some unfortunate tourist being inveigled into having a large and somewhat restless snake wrapped around her shoulders like her best mink is always good for a laugh from her unsympathetic audience . . . until it is their turn . . . but it makes splendid photographs for the 'folks back home'.

Tiger Balm Gardens are at Pasir Panjang, and are far too large ever to move house. The first time I visited Tiger Balm Gardens, I went not knowing quite what to expect. I'd been warned that this was hardly the right place for an impressionable small child, so I'd left my daughter at home. But today's children, brought up on a diet of Dr. Who and Kung Fu would hardly blench at the gaudy conceptions of the terrors which await the ungodly in the afterworld, and indeed would probably enjoy examining the gorier tableau in minute detail. The Gardens have been extended and improved over the years and have a weird and wonderful collection of statues. Some of them are quite ordinary subjects though executed with an oriental flavour. There's even a kind of Disneyland animal kingdom or something remarkably like it with all the creatures springing out of the rock towards one, and a tableau which seems to represent all the strange ones of the Deep, in a dry swimming pool setting, but it is the purely oriental conceptions which are by far the best. Goddesses, Buddhas, giant lotus, gentlemen with Fu Manchu expressions and, right in the centre, the memorials to the two Chinese gentlemen, Messrs Haw and Par, the Aw Brothers who owned the proprietary balm already referred to, and for whom the Gardens are another production, along with its sister in Hong Kong. Singapore's Haw Par Villa, overlooks the sea at Pasir Panjang, but before we step inside (admission is free) let us step back in time to another Chinese merchant who lived in Singapore long before the advent of Mr. Boon Haw and Mr. Boon Par, but who also created a garden.

Hoon Ah Kay was born about 1816 at Whampoa near Canton in China, and in 1830 came to Singapore to join his father in a successful grocery business on the corner of Boat Quay and Telok Ayer Street. After his father's death, Hoon took on the victualling of Naval ships and soon became known as 'Whampoa' to all and sundry. He was particularly popular with the officers of the Navy with whom he came into contact and spoke excellent though sometimes mispronounced English which further endeared him. At first he had a plantation in the Tanglin Area, but later he bought a neglected garden on the Serangoon Road where he built a bungalow and spent huge sums of money on 'improving' the grounds. It became the showplace of the island, called in Cantonese Namsang-fa-un and was visited by the Chinese population at Chinese New Year, when the whole place took on a party atmosphere. But it was also popular with Europeans, for nothing pleased Whampoa more than to put on a show for his friends (in later years he became a CMG and, simultaneously Russian, Chinese and Japanese Consul!). Captain Keppel, whose name is perpetuated in Keppel Harbour, wrote . . .'Whampoa gave sumptuous entertainments. At midnight by the light of a full moon, we would visit the Victoria Regia a magnificent lotus in the circular pond, a present from the Regent of Siam . . . this beautiful flower faced the full moon and moved with it until below the horizon. Among other pets he had an orang-utan, who preferred a bottle of cognac to water. . . .'

When Whampoa died in 1880, his remains were taken back to China and buried on Dane's Island opposite Canton. His obituary columns commented that 'there is not a book of travels touching on Singapore in the last thirty years but mentions the name of Mr. Whampoa.'

I felt that it behoved me to carry on the tradition. After all, the Aw Brothers did.

Today's Singaporeans are also carrying on the traditions of gardens, in spite of losing a great deal of land to the encroachment of living accommodation and industry, necessary though it is. Jurong Bird Garden is a case in point, so let's spare time to go out there and look around. Sightseeing tour buses visit, so do buses and of course, taxis, though this last is fairly expensive as the trip is quite long. On the way you will pass through a number of the new housing estates which have taken over the landscape. Almost the first thing that the foreigner notices about these tall blocks of flats is the bamboo flagpoles which festoon each floor, but on closer inspection the 'flags' prove to be jeans, samfoos, shirts and unmentionables of all kinds. The ever practical Chinese have always used bamboo sticks protruding from their upper windows for personal laundry. Now they've risen several floors, there seems no necessity to change the habits of a lifetime, but I did notice that the newly painted exteriors suffer from the constant drip of water below each window. I suppose one can't have everything. Housing estates in Europe have their shopping areas and their churches. These estates in Singapore have their temples. Toa Payo for instance has a brand new one. It looks a little incongruous to see brand new concrete dragons. Somehow one expects them all to be old and venerable but even dragons have to begin somewhere. There is also a new industrial estate at Jurong. In my day it was all wildland and partly swamp. It has been drained, cleaned and reclaimed and factories and dwellings placed upon it. It thrives, makes money and is a very valuable addition to the island's economy, but it looks disappointingly like industrial Britain with flowers.

The Jurong Bird Park is right in the centre of this 'new'

Singapore, and I was greeted there with a loud wolf whistle. As this is a decidedly rare occurrence I looked around for the perpetrator. I soon found him. A cheeky mynah bird who had been initiated into the ways of man! I tore myself away from the flatterer with some difficulty and hailed one the three trams which trundle around the fifty delightful acres of the park which have been cut from the western slope of Jurong Hill. The tramdriver was a smilingly patient man who stopped obligingly whenever I wanted to rush off and photograph one of his feathered friends. This was very frequently, for the birds are a photogenic lot. Most of them are housed in 78 huge aviaries in conditions closely resembling their natural habitat and giving them masses of room to move safely, but the main feature of Jurong which impressed me very much is the bird equivalent of a safari park. It has a high, giant net stretching between steel cables over five acres of delight – there are tiny red bridges, named romantically Love and Eternity, a suspension bridge spanning the whole aviary, and a man-made waterfall which claims to be the largest of its kind in the world. To attempt to photograph the birds is a long demanding business. Most of the hundreds of species move too swiftly to be captured by the lens, and even the egrets and parakeets skip past one's ear so that one is left with a blur of colour. I decided to make for the peafowls who were wandering more or less aimlessly alongside a path. There were seven peahens in their sombre plumage, and a peacock with his tail dragging behind him. I said 'good afternoon', quite politely and told him he was going to be photographed, and was rewarded with a torrent of unwarranted abuse in his most strident tones, together with a full back view of his immediately erected tail. Trying to get a front view of him presented quite a problem, because each time I moved, he moved as well, shouting his disapproval, while the peahens looked on in shocked silence. Co-operation with the press was something new in a peafowl's existence. It proved a much easier assignment with the flamingos. They went on standing like croquet hoops in their lakes. . . .

The inmates at Tan Moh Hong Crocodile Farm on the upper Serangoon Road were also somewhat easier to photograph than the peacock and not so vociferous but I certainly didn't attempt to get closer to *them*. To reach them, one goes to a typical Singapore house, through a small garden area and out to the enclosures at the rear, where as many as five hundred reptiles are kept, each according to species and age. I cannot honestly say that I liked my companions. It seemed to be mutual. They fixed me with glassy stares as though longing to take a good bite at the hand holding the camera, but I suppose that if one was aware that people only came to visit when interested in the quality of one's skin, or one's dimensions, it might affect one's nature. It is rather like being measured by the undertaker when alive. . . .

The farm has been in existence since 1945, and most of its stock is imported from Indonesia and West Irian. They are fed on prawns and mussels until they are about two feet long. Then they join older relatives, for an earlier introduction would probably mean that they would provide grandpa with a change of diet from pigs' lungs and fish. At about three years old and upwards, selected reptiles are killed off and skinned. I asked how it was accomplished; after all, it isn't exactly like keeping a chicken farm. 'Very quick, very easy' came the reply. 'We hold it by a noose, and put a sharp knife in the brain.' I remembered a similar procedure for killing reindeer in far away Lapland. . . .

There were a number of men in the tanning and curing room, and they showed me how the freshly removed skins are softened in a lime bath and then placed in tanning chemicals in tall earthenware jars. Then, the skin is rubbed steadily on its underside on an adze to soften it in readiness for working into handbags, shoes, etc, or sent for export. They have a number of their own products on sale in the small showroom and the skins are really beautifully cured and worked. But the finish of the articles needs to be improved in comparison with those found in Hong Kong . . . probably made from skins from this very farm! My guide told me that during the 21 years of the firm's existence, lots of celebrities had been to the farm. 'Who for instance?' 'Lord Mountbatten was here. So was Bar-

bara Cartland.' I reflected that it was a rather different visitation than her usual and well-known addiction to the products of the bee.

From the Crocodile Farm, Sheila Yeo and I drove out to Changi. We went along the Tampines Road first, past the fish farms. If you have time in Singapore this is a very pleasant place to spend a morning, particularly if you arrive when the men are netting the fish and moving them from one pond to another in the regular checks on size and condition. But it is not a place which gets into tourist brochures very often, so you would have to ask about getting there. The men use the age old methods of the east, wading into the water, while supervised from a rowing boat, and closing on the fish. They are transfered in batches to other ponds, and this is done almost at a run, the only time I've ever seen locals run in the tropical heat. . . .

We arrived at Changi via the old airport and the former Royal Air Force base, which all looks rather dilapidated these days, though the area will eventually provide the new airport. We passed Changi Gaol too, surely one of the most evocative places for all who remember the dreadful days of 1942-5. So many knew from personal experience just what it was like inside those walls. Men, women and children too, and very much has been written. It wasn't only white Britons who suffered. There were Eurasians, Jews, Tamils, Malays, Javanese, Czechs, Dutch, French, Iraqis and even Germans among the internees. Conditions were terrible but miraculously there developed a cameraderie which became the most powerful force for survival. I was strongly reminded of this when looking through a sketchbook published in 1947, which consists of a series of notes and sketches kept by Iris Parfitt, one of the internees. Again and again I was struck by the fortitude and ingenuity and sense of humour it portrayed. Suffering brings out the best as well as the worst in humanity. On 6th May, 1944, the 3500 civilian internees moved to Sime Road, exchanging places with 2000 POW's and conditions worsened considerably. Looking back it seems incredible that people survived, but many did. For those who did not, there is the great Military memorial out at Kranji, which is a must for those whose loved ones perished in those terrible times. The civilian memorial is on the Padang in Singapore, with the Cenotaph close by, and the memories they evoke are too poignant for comment other than that the debt to them is great.

I wasn't sorry to arrive at Changi beach, where the green sea looked particularly inviting along the narrow sand and a fishing kelong (trap) keeps lonely vigil. These kelongs, standing four-square along all the coasts are a familiar sight. It is possible for visitors to go out to them. At least, it is if one is male. Females aren't too popular as they are considered to bring bad luck on the fishing. So much for Women's Lib. Times are changing slowly. Now it is one of the popular pastimes to hire a kelong for a party, and then a great time is had by all.

We stayed on the beach, paddling in the tepid sea, dreading the moment of returning to the scorching upholstery of the car and trying to ignore the sweat trickling down our backs, but it was really a case of postponing the inevitable. There are a number of small kiosks and restaurants along the beach so after a cold Fanta, a somewhat reluctant pair drove back towards the metropolis. At weekends Changi is a noisy crowded place, but in midweek or in the soft evening cool, it still has a curiously rural air. It won't last when the airport comes. That is why the beaches of St. John's island and elsewhere are being brought more into Singapore's consciousness as places to go. But many, and not just Singaporeans, will remember Changi for their own special reasons, whether happy memories or the sadder, long ago ones. If you do go to the Memorial at Kranji, or go to the Causeway to cross into Johore for some excursion, part of your journey will probably be along the Bukit Timah Road. Now a busy highway, this route has always been an important one right from the beginnings of Singapore's trading and farming history. In the early 1840s, many Chinese had gambier and pepper plantations in this area, but they had great difficulty in persuading coolies to work their crops because of the depredations of tigers, who found the helpless humans all too easy prey. As the jungle was cleared, the hiding places for the fearsome beasts became less, but it took a lot of time. In their splendid book 'One hundred and fifty years of Singapore', Donald and Joanna Moore uncovered a delightful comment on Bukit Timah. Apparently it was considered that this small hill could provide a 'most desirable and agreeable place of residence for the invalids of Singapore were it not that the dwellers on the hill would be exposed to the visitations of tigers . . . occasionally seen and heard on the hill'. The report went on, 'many years must elapse before the island will be cleared and we should much doubt whether the whole of it will ever be so.' I wonder what the would-be crystal-gazer would say today?

For generations before the construction of the Causeway, the only way to cross into Johore was by ferry. In the 1880s there was even talk of a tunnel 'for the purpose of increasing and facilitating the communication between the peoples of two friendly powers'. But it came to nothing and it was not until September 1923 that the Johore Causeway was opened for goods trains. It is a little surprising that Singapore was so go ahead in so many things, but so very backward in others. That this was in part due to the bumbling self-conceit of some of the so-called leaders of the European community is very true, but it would be less than fair to blame them entirely. The wealthy and ruthless in each of the communities were equally culpable. For instance, when looking at the terrible result of the opium trade one must remember that this was carried on by Europeans and Chinese alike. It was profitable, and Singapore was, before anything else, a business-orientated society. It was years before opium smoking was made an offence in Singapore and even then it continued. It still does, though penalties for drug peddling are very heavy in the island today, and can include the death sentence in certain instances.

One of those who was incarcerated in the miseries of Changi Gaol in the Second World War was a certain Dr. G. H. Garlick, a radiologist who was very alive to the scourge of opium. He, and several other internees knew that as and when Singapore was released from Japanese bondage, there was going to be a tremendous incidence of tuberculosis in Singapore.

This disease had been the scourge of Asian peoples, particularly the Chinese, for centuries and one of its root causes was the debilitation caused by constant use of opium. Together with the lack of food, exposure to climatic changes, and the crowded and insanitary conditions in which all the people were living it was bound to exacerbate the problem into a highly dangerous situation. In 1947, under the chairmanship of Mr. S. H. Peck, and who had been, with Dr. Garlick, one of 'the Group' in Changi and Sime Road, an Association was set up, calling itself the Singapore Anti-Tuberculosis Association (SATA), and it started to raise money for X-Ray equipment to find out just how serious the problem was going to be. By 1948 the Clinic was established, and Dr. Garlick became its first full-time radiologist and administrator. Up to that time treatment was either through sanatorium rest or by lung collapse, both of which required more space than SATA had, but the team decided to risk using streptomycin and other very new and comparatively untried drugs on an outpatient basis. At the same time they worked towards their goal of a new diagnostic clinic, and even when I worked there at the end of the fifties, we still had most patients living in their own, often completely inadequate, homes. It was then, for the first time in my life, that I saw just what opium smoking could do to a human being, and it was a lesson that I never forgot. After vicissitudes, the Clinic was opened in Shenton Way by Her Royal Highness Princess Marina, Duchess of Kent, in October 1952, and for years, it was the most modern building in the area, surrounded as it was by many of the old buildings of early Singapore. One of its earliest part time doctors was a certain Dr. Elisabeth Comber. If the name means little to you, I'm not surprised. You would remember her better as Han Suyin.

While on leave in Switzerland in 1958, Dr. Garlick died very suddenly. His ashes were brought back to Singapore for burial in Biddadari Cemetery. Although the good doctor had been a Buddhist for years, it was considered suitable to hold the memorial service in St Andrew's Cathedral, and it was crowded. But it wasn't just the great and important who gathered to pay their respects. The majority of the congregation were the 'little people'. Trishaw drivers, coolies, hawkers and workers of every race to whom Dr. Garlick and his Clinic had brought new life and new hope. It was one of the most moving tributes that I could ever have had the privilege of witnessing. On the day of the service, a strange thing happened. The mail from Europe arrived, and in it was a card, written by Dr. Garlick in Switzerland a few days before his death. He wrote to us that he was sitting on a mountainside and that 'this is a wonderful place in which to say goodbye to the world'. . . .

Now, SATA's pretty little modern building is completely hidden, dwarfed by the forest of new buildings which march all the way along Robinson Road and Shenton Way from Raffles Quay to Anson Road, Keppel Road and the docks. But its work is not dwarfed, though it has changed drastically with the discovery of the drugs which have been instrumental in almost wiping out the scourge of tuberculosis. The Clinic concentrates today on Heart and Cancer work, and it is interesting that with the change of disease, the main source of patients has changed too. They are drawn much more from the Indian community than from the Chinese as hitherto, and perhaps this indicates that diet does affect the incidence of disease far more than most of us realise. SATA still has much to do, but its beginnings are part of the history of the City, and as such, deserved recognition here.

The roads in this district are always very busy, leading as they do, to the constantly busy docks, still the heartbeat of Singapore with the vast PSA Container Port Complex, the oil installations and refineries and bunkering facilities as well as the docks where the cruise ships and lesser fry find their moorings, to say nothing of the constant to-ing and fro-ing of ships in the sea Roads, where it is claimed that a ship enters or leaves approximately every 15 minutes, so one has to allow a little leeway when making appointments. Still it isn't quite as bad as when the dock at Tanjong Pagar was opened in October 1868, when it was recorded that 'there was a traffic jam of carriages and gharries on the road from the town centre'. In the morning rush today, one is inclined to wonder if they've been stuck there ever since. . . . By the way, if you are likely to be in this part of the town at lunchtime, go to the very pleasant restaurant at the Conference Centre. Try Tim Sum, a series of excellent dishes chosen from the trolleys which maintain constant circuit between the tables. Better try to book though, for it is a very popular spot, particularly with business people. Few Europeans seem to go there, or even know it exists, but that is certainly their loss.

With the transformation of Singapore into a city of new high-rise tenement blocks and modern shopping areas, one tends to forget that for generations, most people lived in rather humbler surroundings. It comes as a surprise that in a City which is predominantly Chinese, there is still a district known as Chinatown, but this comes from the days when each race stayed strictly within its own areas. This is breaking down somewhat, as the blocks of flats take people from every part of the community, but there is still a tendency to segregate. It is after all, a natural feeling to be among one's own people, to be within reach of religious buildings that one has known all one's life, and to find the shops which cater for one's own particular needs, as I have said in the Malaysian chapters. But there is no pressure either way, either in Malaysia or in Singapore, by the respective governments. The Chinatown district is crowded, slum property, of which only a few streets remain. Their inmates cling to them with determined desperation, but it can only be a matter of time before they too disappear. I went back to Smith Street to find that my amah's house was shuttered and empty and it is an odd and not very pleasant feeling to know that a little compartment of your life is gone for good. This area is the one for which you will have to make if you want to see anything at all of the old type of shophouses and the hawkers' stalls, and was part of the original area divided into separate sections to cope with the varying races from China. Many of the hawkers have disappeared into the maw of the People's Markets across busy New Bridge Road, but there will be more than enough for you to find all the sights, scents and sounds that one associates with the 'mysterious Orient', and you will find that each lane has its own trades. Lanterns hang on long poles like sections of white slug, waiting to be transformed with handpainting, along with magnificently formed papier mache heads, used at carnivals, dragon dances, etc. Next come the undertakers and funeral furnishings, not the dull, stark things that we supply, but far more intricate. The Chinese always bury a man with enough possessions to give him status in the next world. But they are a people drilled in centuries of frugality. All the possessions therefore, are in paper . . . houses, furniture, boats, money, even concubines, and they are burned in ceremony 100 days after the death. You will find yourself in Sago Lane. This street used to contain the death houses, though these are fast becoming things of the past and are used more as funeral parlours these days. The phrase 'death house', evokes a terrible picture of a fearsome place. How did it start?

Chinese are also gregarious. Many of the poor lived, as we can see from these few mean streets, in extremely crowded conditions, in premises owned by often unscrupulous landlords. They still do, despite the rigid laws on overcrowding in government houses, laid down as long ago as British rule. They are also highly superstitious, and many of the landlords considered that it was 'bad joss' – bad luck – for someone to die in their house, and a family could face eviction if an old or sick person lived in their midst. Because of this, it became the custom for the dying to be put into separate houses, with the family paying for maintenance and visiting when possible. When working for SATA, it was often the case that the only bed we could get for a patient was in a death house, whether he was beyond help or not. The rooms were always crowded and very sad to me, but not frightening, and were usually as clean as the confined space could allow. Since that time, I have seen a great deal of old people's homes in Britain, and I've seen the same expressions on the faces. It is a kind of inevitability that tears the heart.

Slum housing was quite different. It was awful and I am glad that so much has gone. Few Europeans ventured within. I was privileged by my badge, and was always received kindly, allowed in past the fierce looking men at the doors, and a stool set for me. I'll remember one woman always. She lived in unbelievably squalid conditions in a kind of cupboard, with four children. She had advanced tuberculosis, and we had an opportunity to get her into hospital, but she refused to go. 'This bad place, a lot of gangsters,' she said through my interpreter. 'If I go hospital nobody look after children. I stay'. . . and she did.

Gangs have always been a menace in the Chinese social pattern. Secret Societies came from China in the early days, bringing all the hatreds and rivalries with them, and caused very many of the frightful riots which killed hundreds and injured hundreds more innocent people. It is impossible to ignore riots when reading or writing of Singapore's history, for every now and then they have flared without seeming reason and they have been ugly blotches on the City's skin. One hopes that they are a thing of the past, but Secret Societies are still strong. Only a few months ago, I read an account in a Bangkok newspaper of one of them, which was using an old Chinese cemetery at Pek San Teng to run gambling schools, samsu (illicit liquor) distilleries, blue film clubs and protection rackets to gamblers and villagers alike. The cemetery was originally chosen because superstitious Chinese camped out there in the hope that the dead would bring them luck and reveal lucky numbers in local lotteries, and the underworld cashed in on it. A new town in the area might dislodge all the gangsters, but apparently not all the local residents think along those lines. Their great-grandfathers lived there, they say. And how would they keep a pig and chickens in a highrise flat? These are the questions that Singapore has to answer every day. The people in Chinatown too, cling to the buildings they've known all their lives, unwilling to change the known discomforts for new ways of life, however seemingly preferable. But change they must. The Singapore Government is determined on that.

Keep a look-out in the poorer districts for the calligraphists. The art is dying out now and there aren't many of their breed, but every so often, tucked away under the dark shadow of a verandahed street you will find one, perched on a small stool, bent over a portable desk, carefully gold lettering some ribbon of red paper, or listening to a client's instructions. Most of their customers are of the China-born generation, wanting to write back to relations in Mainland China or in Hong Kong and wishing to use the old-fashioned phrases which are fast disappearing from common usage, but who are probably not literate enough to write for themselves. The calligraphist will write for them, charging perhaps one or two dollars per letter. But, in addition, he does a tremendous trade in good luck papers which are particularly popular at Chinese New Year and at weddings. You'll see some of these pinned on the wall above his head and if you want to buy one it costs according to the number of characters used. Happy New Year, or Double Happiness, will cost a dollar, and you'll go away the proud possessor of something which belongs among the oldest customs in Singapore. The more modern calligraphists can be seen around the Supreme Court or police station, complete with typewriters. They will write business letters for less lettered brethren, but the 'red paper man' is unique and well worth searching for.

Search for the fortune tellers too. These sometimes operate through cards and will tell your future for a small fee. But the most entertaining to watch are the ones who train a small bird to pick out a 'fortune' for you. The main forecast is usually very similar. You are going to be lucky, healthy, but you'll have to work hard. But the bird does its best to be impartial. There are also a number of street doctors, selling patent medicines and cure-alls which still have a place in Old Singapore. I've seen them operating many a time, but the best I ever saw was in Sabah, so I've included him in that chapter. But you'll find lots like him in the Lion City and elsewhere in Malaysia too for that matter, if you look hard.

The food markets are remarkable, and varied. Dried frogs, peculiar sausages, monkey brains, python meat, live turtles, chickens and rabbits, all wait side by side for the housewives, neat in their cool, flowered, high-buttoned, wide-legged trouser suits called samfoo, and the blue-clad older generations with immaculate hair and gold teeth. If you are squeamish, don't go in search of the python lady. She skins a snake while you wait, chopping it into pieces with an indifference born of long usage, but her *piece de resistance* is de-shelling turtles. One would never drink turtle soup again if watching this performance and going straight for lunch. . . . There are chestnut vendors, mee sellers, fruit hawkers, all cheek by jowl in an unbelievably congested area, but they are all fascinating and the time flies. One of my favourites, is the brushseller. His stall is a bicycle with carefully built mountain of brushware which would do credit to the Kleen-e-zee man. It quite dwarfs him and how on earth he sees around it, let alone cycles on the main road, I'll never know. All of it is so photogenic that one hardly knows where to begin, and usually it is fairly easy to photograph if one is quick about it. But do remember that many of the older generations believe that a photograph imprisons the soul and are not too keen on tourists taking pictures of them. On one occasion, I was trying to take pictures of a dear little old lady as she deftly cut pineapples into strips, when she spotted me. She lifted her parang so threateningly that I fled, much to the amusement of my Indian friend, and the imprecations followed me right across the road and into the People's Park.

Another 'must' in your crowded few days is a visit to Thieves Market, open in the afternoons in a straggle of streets beside the Rochore Canal. This hotch potch of stalls and small shops stacked with *bric-a-brac* and antiques of all description is a marvellous excursion into a Singapore which is fast fading from sight. Leave jewellery and valuables locked up in the hotel safe for this trip, but take some money with you, because you are bound to find something interesting and/or cheaper than elsewhere. The fact that it is probably (a) counterfeit, (b) smuggled (c) has 'fallen off the back of a lorry' or a combination of all three should be taken into consideration and bargaining is essential. The secret of this delightful exercise is to take your time, not to show interest in the piece you want to buy, and finally when you are getting into the region of the price you want to pay, walk away. If the seller doesn't call you back, you've got a bargain. On the other hand, he just might be sharper than you are! The story goes that many Singaporeans went to Thieves Market daily after the Japanese occupation, to buy back their own property, or that of their friends, which had been looted indiscriminately. I am assured, on the best authority, that many Europeans refurnished their homes with their *own* possessions that way.

Change Alley, a narrow noisy thoroughfare running between the high buildings of Collier Quay and Raffles Place is, in my opinion, overrated and distinctly touristy, but you should run its gauntlet at least once. C. K. Tangs, in Orchard Road, known and patronised by generations of expatriates is always worth a look. The shop hasn't always been there. For years, it occupied scruffy little premises in River Valley Road, and one entered through long bamboo curtains into a veritable Aladdin's Cave, where delicate vases perched perilously on pyramids of dusty teak or rosewood furniture, and embroidered slippers seemed to grow in piles beside grotesque carved masks, porcelain dogs and bamboo trays. When the shop moved, out of sheer necessity for greater space, to the opulent building in Orchard Road, in 1958-9, it lost some of its charm, but one still found many beautiful things within the red laquered doors. Now, it has degenerated somewhat into more of an emporium, supplying everyday things on its upper floors instead of its magnificent array of furniture, but I have a soft spot for Tangs, and always try there first for most requirements.

There are almost too many alternatives when it comes to shopping. If you are looking for jewellery, it might be an idea to go to the dozens of Chinese gold shops in South Bridge Road. You will have to argue prices, and you will find that some might not understand English, but it is worth while, and when you do find items you want, you may be sure they are real. They'll weigh the gold for you, and meticulously list the whole purchase. Now, they all use electronic calculators, which is rather disappointing. Before the invention of these gadgets, the abacus could be heard clicking the fortunes of the jewellers all day long, and when the newcomers first made their appearance, there were competitions between old and new methods for counting in which the old always won. But times change. . . . If you hate bargaining choose one of the endless tourist shops in Orchard Road, or an expensive jewellers. As always in Singapore, it is your choice. Cameras, tape-recorders and all the other expensive gadgetry that come with modern living can be bought by the ton. Everyone will tell you that his favourite store is the best and I am no exception, but I've long learned that one man's meat . . . so if you find an article you like, at a price you think right, then you have your bargain. If not, leave it and go elsewhere.

Most male visitors rush off to get shirts and suits made in incredibly short periods of time, and it is amusing to see every European man in Orchard Road carrying an unmistakable parcel containing all these goodies. The same facilities are of course, available for ladies and Chinese dressmakers are also skilful in copying a favourite dress in local materials. Khersonese silk is making an appearance now. This is an entirely local product, but in the Indian shops in the vicinity of High Street you'll find any and every variety of fabric, and touts will assure you at each door of a 'special price for you'. It will take time if the women members of the party are let loose here, so the men might like to move on a little. The City Hall, facing the Padang, will probably revive a few nostalgic memories for older visitors who were in the Armed Services. The entrance to the Surrender Chamber is beneath the main steps, and there is a comprehensive display of maps, photographs, waxworks and sound and light performances. All deal with the Second World War, from the surrender of the Commonwealth Forces in February 1942 to the total surrender of the Japanese in South-East Asia which took place in this very room on 12th September 1945. It is well worth spending time to go there, whether you are of a generation that remembers that War or not.

Going back further in time to Raffles again, you'll find a statue of him in Empress Place. Another marks his landing spot, although it is supposed that he made his first landing on Singapore Island on the river bank somewhere here, between what used to be known as Hallpike's boatyard and the Marine Police Station. I have no precise and reliable information on fixing the exact spot. One old reference book says that for the four years subsequent to the establishment of the settlement, the Temenggong and his followers occupied the stretch of the river bank inland to where the bridge stands in North Bridge Road. He may have withdrawn a short distance up river after the British party arrived. But even if he didn't, it is reasonable to assume that Raffles and Farquhar came ashore a little to the seaward side, so we must be close to their footsteps here. Back along Collier Quay where traffic is heavy enough to warrant an overhead crossing. This one is complete with a shopping complex, but before mounting into its intricacies, spare a glance at the Fullerton Building on the corner of Fullerton Square. This marks the site of the former Fort Fullerton which protected old Singapore. Across the square is the Asia Insurance Building, and there is a tragic little story attached to it. For years, from morning to night, a tiny Chinese woman stood looking up at the building, raising her fists and cursing it aloud, while the uncaring world whizzed by. It appears that her son had been working on the construction of the Asia Building when he fell to his death. . . . She isn't there now, but I spoke to many people who saw her, as I did. She was, foı her lifetime, one of the fixtures of Singapore, and at least, on this page, we can remember her, and her sorrow.

All the while you walk these crowded streets, you'll be conscious of the many religions and beliefs which surround you, alien to your own, but with a tremendous fascination, and probably engendering a longing to know a little more. Temples are legion. One can hardly turn a corner in older districts without finding an open door, leading to a courtyard and buildings where people pursue their various faiths. Taoists, Buddhists, Hindus, Catholics, Moslems, all have their own place and their own beauty, and there have been days when, within the space of a few hours, I have seen ceremonies in all of them. In consequence, one is strongly reminded that Belief is important, and that difference is often a matter of degree. Naturally enough, it is the colour and exoticism which appeal to the senses of a European in the East, and therefore it is the Taoist, Buddhist and Hindu which provide the most interesting and unusual sightseeing interludes. Taoist temples are the most accommodating. No-one ever minds the advent of visitors, as long as they behave with decorum, and there are no particularly strict rules to observe. Note that you usually have to place your foot over a highish wooden division to enter the inner regions. This provides the necessary bowing movement to give respect, as the body moves naturally to keep balance. In the vicinity of Sago Lane, you'll find the little Sian Hian temple, one of the oldest in Singapore. Many women go there to pray for fertility so joss burns constantly. A little further away in Telok Ayer Street, is Tian Hock Keng. Used by the Hokkien Chinese mostly, the temple images and stonework were all brought from China in the mid-nineteenth century.

Along South Bridge Road is Sri Mariamnan, the Hindu temple. You can't miss it, because its entrance is pyramid shaped and gaudily decorated and carved. The most exciting time to visit is during the fire-walking ceremonies, in which the pits are full of live coals, and the devotees cross them apparently without pain or scars, due to their exalted condition. If you are unlikely to be at the Batu Caves in Kuala Lumpur at the festival of Thaipusam, but you can get to Singapore, you can follow all the rituals by watching the beginning of the ceremonies at the Perumal Temple in Serangoon Road, or you could be present at the finale at the Subramanian Temple in Tank Road. (Lord Subramania is the embodiment of virtue, youth, bravery and beauty and his place in the hierarchy is that of son to the Great Siva). This temple is also known as the Chettiars Temple, because it was built by the money-lenders just over 100 years ago. These, as any former resident in Singapore can vouch, are part and parcel of the life of many of the inhabitants. It used to be a common sight for me to watch employees at Paya Lebar vaulting over back fences on payday and belting off across country to avoid the waiting pack at the Airport gate! I suppose it will always be part of humanity's pattern that man lives above his income, whether rich or poor. Whatever, and however, it was built, Chettiars Temple is one of the most tranquil places in the city on the days when there are none of the emotional ceremonies inspired by Thaipusam. One morning, two monks sat on the shaded verandahs when I visited. They were threading fragrant frangipani flowers into garlands in readiness for the day's devotions and greeted me courteously as they worked. I sat down beside them on the cool stones, and our conversation was of religion, politics, and the world situation, and, as the heady perfume wafted across us and the heap of garlands grew, we put our world to rights. But one remark stayed longest in my mind. 'When a married man dies,' said one of my mentors, 'he is buried with full honours. You see, he has given of himself and taken on the responsibilities of others. A single man has not done that, and therefore, he is buried without ceremony. People must have responsibility. That is their task in life'.

In Racecourse Road is the Buddhist Temple of a Thousand Lights. It has a magnificent 50 foot statue of Buddha, framed in electric lights, hence its name. It also contains a mother of pearl replica of Buddha's footprint, a tableau of his life, and a piece of bark from the Bodhi tree. Vesak Day ceremonies are during the first week of May, and celebrate the ascension of Lord God Buddha to Heaven. This is the time to see the temple at its best, when thousands of believers fill the halls, the gongs sound and the bells fill the air. I was invited for the ceremonies once on that day, and afterwards we went into the cool refectory to sit at long bare tables for tea. The little sticky cakes were typical of many I had tasted in the East, but the tea was like no other I have tasted, either before or since. Nectar of the God indeed. But tea, or no tea, it was a most impressive and beautiful ceremonial on that Vesak Day, which again strengthened my belief that God has many faces to the peoples on His planet.

Before leaving the Lion City completely, it would be a pity not to try to visit some of the little islands which belong to her territory. Most are attractive, some are historic, and many are certainly worth visiting. They provide excellent opportunities for swimming and sunbathing, though extra care must be taken in these exposed places. New holiday playgrounds are being built on the island now, and by the time this book is published some, apart from the already mentioned Sentosa, will be in full use. But there is more than a holiday image, however enticing. Beyond Pulau Bukum, is Pulau Hantu, known for centuries as Ghost Island to the Malays. Legend has it that two warlords were killed and buried there and that their ghosts haunt the place. Certainly there are two tombstones of uncertain origin. St. John's was a leper colony and an internment centre before taking up its present purpose as a tourist complex, but beyond St. John's are the Sisters. These are usually crowded with picnickers and, when the tide is low, you can wade from one to the other (use sandals in these waters, to avoid standing on a coral or stinging fish). Kusu, near to Lazarus Island, contains a Chinese Taoist Temple dedicated to the God of Prosperity, Tua Pek Kong, and during its festival the island is thronged with worshippers. Also on this island is a Muslim kramat, so quite obviously it has been a holy place for generations. Its legend confirms this, because it tells of a giant turtle who saved the lives of shipwrecked sailors in wild seas by turning itself into the present island. The Orang Laut (sea people) lived for generations in this area, and I once had the privilege of attending a Bersanding of the daughter of the chief on Lazarus Island. I was taken to meet the little bride, incarcerated in a tiny room inside one of the stilt houses. Beads of perspiration were running down her face while the ladies of the house dressed her in her wedding baju sarong. Her fingertips had already been stained with henna as a sign of forthcoming marriage and, as I passed through the main room of the house, the finishing touches were being given to the dais. This contained a throne, covered entirely in pink satin cushions and curtains in readiness for the 'reception'. Outside in the village street, long trestle tables were placed under palm leaf awnings for the wedding feast, already giving forth the most exquisite curry smells. The Bersanding takes place in the afternoon, and in the morning, the bridegroom entertains guests at his home until it is time to go in procession to his bride's home, complete with band. At 'our' wedding, on arrival at the house, he had to pay a small sum of money at each door leading to the room where the dais was placed, and again when he took his place beside his bride. She was now wearing a very pretty flowered and gilded head--dress, and he was in the full glory of 'kain songket' baju, trousers and sarong, with a ceremonial ornamental kris at his waist. The happy pair sat, without a smile, very upright on their throne, all through the prolonged ceremonies (in older times, I was told, the bride had to keep her eyes lowered as well!). There were mounds of cooked yellow rice and red-dyed eggs, scattered with a mass of flower blossoms, the band played, verses from the Koran were read, and then off they all went in procession to the bridegroom's house for the whole perfomance all over again. We, accompanied by the entire village, or so it seemed, tucked into the waiting curry, complete with coconuts fetched down from the trees by an obliging baboon. It was a wonderful affair, but I didn't want to see curry again for days!

While I cannot guarantee you a wedding, nor indeed any of the other many ceremonies I have described (for such opportunities come only once in a lifetime, and I have been blessed) you can at least hope to see some of them. Launches and sampans will take you out to many of these lovely little islands from Clifford Pier, and in addition there are special tourist launches which undertake day cruises and you might prefer these. But be careful of the ultraviolet rays, even if it is overcast. Take Singapore gently as she deserves, and she will come up to every one of your expectations and give much in return.

What of the future for this island in the sun? I think she can manage her own destiny very well, provided she is left in peace to get on with it under her undoubtedly talented leader. Long may he be able to help to guide her, but even so, the people are a disciplined, sensible community. They have many problems, they work hard .. too hard sometimes, they play hard also, and most of them live well. New laws seem to come into force daily, which perhaps can in time lead to over-organisation, and local people grumble. But they obey, hoping that the general prosperity which has been theirs for so long will continue, and they know that much which has been done could never have been accomplished without that constant exhortation. They hope that in time, relaxation will be greater, but they know only too well that there are many dangers on their doorstep. I hope, for them, that they will never be challenged by them, and that Singapore will long be the peaceful magnet which draws so many people to this intriguing corner of South East Asia.

Recipes from Malaysia and Singapore.

Fish and Pork Dish (from the Chinese Chef at the E and O Hotel Penang)

Ingredients
One large thick plaice or sole.
Several very thin slices of streaky or, if preferred, lean pork.
Chinese or fresh mushrooms.
Root ginger.
Garlic to taste.
One teaspoon of oil
One tablespoon of brandy
Salt and pepper.

Slice ginger very thinly into strips. Slice mushrooms. Place all ingredients on a deepish fireproof plate and place over steamer. Cover and cook for twenty minutes (cooking for longer loses the flavour).
Important. Add no water to ingredients. Serve immediately. Dish should not start to cook before first course is commenced, so that no overcooking will take place.

2. **Satay Gravy** (from Jasmine, at the Merlin Beach Club, Penang)

Ingredients
Ground Peanuts
Spices (jintan manis – can be bought from Indian or Eastern stores)

Dried chili, pounded to soften.
Garlic to taste
Onion chopped
Oil for cooking
Ground coconut, made into paste and gently fried.
Juice of tamarind if available.
Root ginger.

Fry chili for ten minutes in oil, adding onions, garlic, spices. Then add tamarind juice and coconut. Simmer for five minutes very gently. Add peanuts. Cook very gently for about 45 minutes.
Use over meatballs, or with satay sticks etc.

3. **Spiced Mutton Chops** (from Ujagar Singh Restaurant, Singapore)

Ingredients
1 lb lamb chops (mutton will suffice)
Small piece root ginger, finely chopped.
1 lb fresh tomatoes, quartered
Several small chopped onions.
Garlic to taste.
Green chili chopped into four.
Curry powder . . . one heaped teaspoon.
a little red chilli powder, salt and pepper to taste.

Place all ingredients in heavy pan with lid. Add just enough water to prevent sticking. Simmer, stirring occasionally, until all the liquid has dried, and chops are cooked. Before serving fry chops for a few moments on both sides. Serve with lettuce, slices of lemon, and mint chutney.

4. **Singapore Gin Sling** (traditional method – Originated in 1915 in Raffles Hotel)

Ingredients
2 measures Gin
1 measure Cherry Brandy

1 measure fresh orange, lemon and pineapple juice.
Drop of Angostura bitters.
Drop of Cointreau.

Shake well with ice and serve in tall glass, garnished with pineapple and cherry.

5. **Gula Melaka** (generally used in Malaysia and Singapore)

Ingredients
6 oz Sago
6 oz dark brown sugar
2 thin slices fresh ginger
6 oz coconut milk (may be made from coconut cream, bought in blocks, in U.K.)
Pinch of salt.

Wash sago, pour into pan and cover with water. Boil until sago becomes clear. Sieve and rinse under running water to remove starch. Place in mould to set. Place sugar in pan, with half pint water and boil. Add ginger slices and cook until sugar is syrup. Cool. Mix coconut milk with salt and chill. To serve, put sago into individual bowls and pour on coconut milk and syrup to taste.

Finally, a recipe of a different kind . . . if you can stomach the smell, do try the durian fruit when it is in season. That is, if you want to find out the truth of the old Malay proverb which, when translated, says. . . . When durian comes down, sarongs go up. . . . It could quite equally apply to other nationalities as well. . . .

Index

Malaysia